IN THEIR OWN WORDS

In Their Own Words

UNTOLD STORIES OF THE FIRST WORLD WAR

Anthony Richards

Published by IWM, Lambeth Road, London SE1 6HZ
IWM.ORG.UK

© The Trustees of the Imperial War Museum, 2016

ISBN 978–1–904897–53–8

A catalogue record for this book is available from the
British Library
Printed and bound by CPI Group (UK) Ltd, Croydon, CR0 4YY

All images © IWM unless otherwise stated
Front cover: Q 24069 (artificially coloured)
Back cover: Q 54352

Every effort has been made to contact all copyright holders.
The publishers will be glad to make good in future editions any error
or omissions brought to their attention.

10 9 8 7 6 5 4 3 2 1

Contents

Introduction

Over the last few decades, the presentation of history to the wider public through museums, publications and the media has seen an increasing prominence given to eyewitness accounts. This development is particularly obvious when we look at the many and varied interpretations of the First World War. We enjoy learning from the experiences of our ancestors, but while the unit war diaries, military orders and memoranda in the care of the National Archives portray the official narrative, we need to look elsewhere in order to understand the more human side of conflict. As the events of 1914 to 1918 grow more distant, and surviving participants of the war have gradually disappeared, we have witnessed a much greater reliance on recorded first-hand testimony to tell us exactly what it was like to experience those critical events.

While many published memoirs had already appeared in the 1920s and 1930s which supplied individual recollections, by the 1960s there was still no comprehensive archival source which could provide a broad range of personal evidence. A resurgence of public interest in the Great War had resulted in part from the popularity of the BBC's ground-breaking 1964 documentary series of that name, as well as the recent release by the Public Record Office (PRO) of the official papers concerning the conflict. Mindful of this, and also perhaps of the impending release of Second World War material at the PRO, the then-Director of the Imperial War Museum (IWM),

Dr Noble Frankland, argued that historians would enjoy a better understanding of these two great events if they could also have ready access to the personal papers kept by actual participants.

A new IWM Documents Section was therefore created in 1969, charged with building up an archive of largely unpublished letters, diaries and memoirs written by servicemen and women since 1914, as well as civilians during wartime. The few hundred manuscripts that the Documents Section inherited from the museum's library, which had been collecting unpublished material in a small way since IWM's foundation in 1917, soon grew into an extensive collection. By the time of the Centenary of the First World War, the archive embraced the papers of well over 20,000 individuals from Britain and its former Empire, and continues to be developed through regular donations and bequests.

The strength of IWM's Documents collection lies in its breadth of coverage, as it includes the writings of individuals from many varied backgrounds. Indeed, it was one of IWM's founding principles in 1917 that the museum should chronicle the experiences of ordinary people. Modern wars are fought and experienced at different levels, and the personal records of regular men and women are therefore treated equally to those of senior commanders or key decision-makers. The correspondence, diaries and reminiscences in the museum's care contain not only compelling first-hand descriptions of the events witnessed, but also reveal the writers' personal thoughts on the issues raised by war.

Those papers relating to the First World War are a particularly essential resource. This book brings together, for the first time, 11 key stories from the collection. From Rosie Neal's patriotic pluck when escaping the enemy's homeland at the outbreak of the conflict, to Gilbert Laithwaite's anxiety at attempting to survive the most intense German assault of the war in March 1918, the personal accounts which form the core of this book are the most direct way in which we can now experience those world-shattering events

– through the words of those who were actually there. For that reason, IWM's collection is now one of the most important archives anywhere in the world for those seeking to examine the impact of modern war on British society.

Unless another source is cited, the information contained in each chapter is taken directly from the letters, diary or memoir written by the person in question. Every effort has been made to check historical accuracy, but when an error has been made by the original author (most commonly of a very minor nature and due to the passage of time) this has been noted. The original quotations have, only where necessary, been lightly edited in terms of punctuation and spelling but overall remain as written by each individual. For those interested to read the original (and in some cases significantly longer) accounts, I would encourage you to do so by booking an appointment to visit the IWM Research Room. See iwm.org.uk for further details.

Acknowledgements

This has been my first book and, as such, I have relied on a number of people to guide me through the process. Firstly, and where else would I list them, Natasha and Henry have been incredibly supportive. I will always be grateful to Liz Bowers who, in her role as IWM Head of Publications, had faith in me as an author and believed that this book would be a worthwhile project. The current IWM Publications team have also offered much help, with particular recognition going to Caitlin Flynn. I would like to thank Miranda Harrison for her editing and Roger Smither for reading the manuscript. The relatives of those whose accounts form the basis of this book have been extremely kind in allowing me to publish their words, and particular appreciation goes to Margaret Woodley and Kit Hesketh-Harvey; Fanny Hugill and Caroline Ryder; the President and Fellows of Trinity College, Oxford; Denis Caslon; Felix Gameson; Tim Le Grice; and Sarah West (whose own book based on Gabrielle West's diaries is due for publication in 2016).

Within the museum, I feel it is only right to single out two particular individuals for special thanks. Peter Hart (punk star, best-selling author and battlefield guide) shared an enormous amount of advice with me during his rare visits to IWM, where he occasionally works as an oral historian. Peter read through an early draft of the book and his constructive criticism was greatly appreciated; any errors remaining are purely my own. I would also like to thank the museum's Queen of Communications, Lucy Donoughue, for her much-appreciated encouragement throughout the writing of this book. In fact, the book would almost certainly never have happened in the first place if it wasn't for her nudging me in the right direction, for which I will be eternally thankful (if a little bruised).

Finally, I should like to acknowledge two individuals who are sadly no longer with us. My father Peter Richards died shortly before I signed the contract for this book, but in one of our final conversations I was able to confirm that it was definitely happening, which I think pleased him greatly. Should he have had the opportunity to read the book, I think he would have enjoyed it. I hope that the same could be said of Rod Suddaby, my predecessor as Head of IWM's Documents collection. He worked incredibly hard for many decades in building up and maintaining an archive of immense international importance, and in a small way this published collection of stories can be seen as a tribute to his dedication.

I | Rosie

OUTBREAK OF WAR
AUGUST 1914

The war had begun and my heart beat then as it had never beaten before

In the manner of local newspapers the world over, at the beginning of the twentieth century the *Edinburgh Evening News* was publishing regular reviews of theatrical shows appearing in its district. The edition for 31 October 1905 contained a typical example, featuring John Henry Cooke's Circus – a place of entertainment that had 'opened its house for the season last night with a programme which, for all round excellence and variety, has never been excelled'. The Circus was known for its various equestrian acts, which included Miss Marie Meers, billed as 'England's neatest and prettiest exponent of the Newmarket Jockey', while Mademoiselle Ada Marjutti, described as 'The Flexible Venus', 'more than justified her title by her wondrous performance in this particular line'. The most novel feature of the evening was a troupe of Cingalese performers who gave an exhibition of native dancing with an accompaniment of 'wailing melodies, the jingling of an instrument which they carried, and the beating of a barrel drum'. Also appearing on the bill were The Five Brewsters, an all-girl act who combined singing, playing and dancing, and whom the *Edinburgh Evening News* considered 'an enjoyable turn'.

Also known as The Brewster Troupe or The Royal Brewsters, the girls were led by Katherine Neal who, under the stage name of Kitty Brewster, had enjoyed success as a Victorian music hall artist. According to family legend, her surrogate father had taught Queen Victoria how to play the banjo. Joining Kitty in the troupe were her younger sister, Rosie, and three other girls. Regular tours of theatres and music halls, with their entertaining mixture of singing and dancing, had brought considerable success. By the summer of 1914 the troupe was ready to embark on a month-long theatrical tour of Germany, beginning with a date in Hamburg on 1 August. For the 22 year-old Rosie and her young friends, a trip which promised to deliver the fun, glamour and excitement associated with a European jaunt would, in the event, prove disastrous.

The five members of the Brewster Troupe arrived in Hamburg at 6.00am, early in the bitterly cold Monday morning of 27 July. Rosie had suffered sea-sickness during the voyage, which perhaps had been influenced by the weather; recent days had been unusually cold, considering that this time of year would normally be considered high summer. Eventually the ship was towed in to the docks and the girls disembarked, carrying their hand luggage to the custom house, which was no short distance. Kitty, benefitting from her position as troupe leader, elected to wait for the main luggage to be unloaded from the ship while Rosie and her friend Edie were sent off to look for accommodation.

We settled our rooms, after asking the landlady if she thought we wanted to buy the house, and returned to the custom house only to find that the luggage had been lost. What consternation there was for a time, all the theatre stuff lost, over £300 worth, what should we do if we couldn't get it before 1st August? But needless to say we did find it, although not for hours. We went all over the town, back again to the ship, and the captain informed us it was not there. So we sent a telegram to England. About mid-day we met a man in the street who informed us our luggage was found, for it was still on the ship. We breathed a sigh of relief, as we made our way to the docks once more. We arrived at our rooms having done all the work, feeling quite pleased with ourselves for the remainder of that day.

The following day was a more sedate one as the girls recovered from their voyage and occupied themselves with pleasant thoughts, enjoying their new surroundings and planning their stay in Hamburg. In the evening Rosie accompanied Kitty and Edie for a walk, during which they called at a cafe for a drink.

While sitting there, all the newspaper boys began to shout at once 'England and Germany'. Not being able to stand this any longer we asked the waiter what it all meant. He, either being too upset or not able to understand my good German, could tell us nothing, so we came to our own conclusion that there was going to be a war, at which we gave a hearty laugh, strolled home, had our supper and turned into bed feeling quite easy about the war.

It is perhaps forgivable that the girls showed little concern for the likelihood of a war occurring between Britain and Germany. Those who had been keeping a closer eye on political and military current affairs, however, might have been more prepared for a violent outcome to the summer's crisis.

The political situation across Europe had been thrown into turmoil by the assassination of Archduke Franz Ferdinand, heir to the Austrian throne, shot during an official visit to the Bosnian capital Sarajevo on Sunday 28 June. The gunman was one Gavrilo Princip, a member of the secret Serbian society known as The Black Hand, which had been formed to promote the political and racial unification of Serbia with the Slav populations in Bosnia, Austria-Hungary and other neighbouring territories. Their ultimate goal was the formation of a new Yugoslavian state. The Austro-Hungarian Empire had controversially annexed Bosnia and Herzegovina in

1908, taking over its significant number of Slavic inhabitants and in the process seriously damaging relations with Serbia and its close ally, the Russian Empire.

Austria-Hungary blamed the Serbian government for supporting the assassination of Franz Ferdinand, but the strong links between Serbia and Russia meant that any threat to the smaller country would likely lead to larger repercussions. Austria therefore fell back on support from her strongest ally, Germany. Russia maintained an informal alliance with France, as did Britain; this European balance of power had been regarded as a way to guarantee peace and avoid any major conflict within central Europe, despite the constant 'troubles' present in the Balkans. It is perhaps ironic, therefore, that in the subsequent 'July Crisis', these beneficial ties would fast become the chains that would drag each and every one of the chief European powers into a major war.

The Austrian demand for revenge on Serbia coincided with a degree of opportunism on behalf of the other nations involved, but particularly in the case of Germany. The German Empire was already building up its military and naval force to exert power, but the instability caused by the assassination suddenly presented a new opportunity. As international tensions developed, basic preparations for war by all countries began across Europe, with military strategies revised and mobilisation of armies planned in order to make a clear statement to one's rivals. Even before the events of Sarajevo, a war in Europe had been considered likely by many commentators.

Although Serbia suggested international arbitration to resolve the matter, Austria-Hungary severed diplomatic communications and declared war on Serbia on Tuesday 28 July. The following day, Germany requested a guarantee of British neutrality in the event of war, which was refused by the Foreign Secretary, Sir Edward Grey. Russia ordered full mobilisation on 31 July, as did Austria and Turkey, with Germany, France and Belgium following suit on Saturday 1 August.

For Rosie and her friends, however, the only event to arouse excitement in their minds on this particular Saturday would most likely have been their imminent performance to entertain the theatre-going public of Hamburg. There was a distinct lack of information available to non-German speakers, as the local newspaper sellers were no longer supplying English papers. Post from England was not being delivered either, and so the girls had stopped writing home. They intended to return in a few days, at any rate, and would have ample opportunity to catch up with world events once their tour was over.

That same morning, August 1st, our landlady informed us her nephew was coming and would want our room (mine and Edie's – we didn't live at the same house as Kitty and the two other girls as there was no room, so we were obliged to sleep out). She told us that Kitty's landlady had another room now and it would be much nicer for us all to be in the same house. She would help us move our clothes and baskets. We thought her a very nice woman and I tell you we were jolly sorry to leave, but it is only now that we know that she was a wicked old bounder. She had heard the rumours of the war and wouldn't have us in her house as we were English. Anyway, Kit's landlady took us in and was jolly pleased to.

Evening arrived and the girls began to get ready for their show. Unfortunately their excitement and anticipation would be spoiled by the first inklings of war reaching out to touch their lives.

When night came round we set off extra light-hearted to work but, alas, there we sat and waited. Presently one man came in, who enquired if there wasn't going to be a show. The manager had to tell him that he didn't think so, as he was the only audience that had made an appearance and it was then ten o clock, so there we sat far into the night talking of the war. We returned home feeling very downhearted as the war was the cause of no audience and no show. That night the last ship sailed for home, but we didn't know it.

The following day was Sunday 2 August. Unbeknown to the girls, German troops were marching into Russian Poland, Luxembourg and France. The girls discussed what they should do and came to the realisation that even if the theatre were to open, the audience were unlikely to accept a troupe of English girls performing for them. They therefore looked at the possibility of finishing their tour early, and discovered that no ships were leaving for England. Dutifully returning to the theatre that evening, they found the building locked up and decided that the only thing to do would be to report to the British Consulate first thing in the morning.

So when Monday came round we went, and to our great surprise there were hundreds of English people in that office. Eventually we were able to speak to the Consul and we told our troubles as hundreds had done that same morning. We told him that we had come over here to work a month at the theatre but now the place was closed and the director gone to the war, we had our return tickets, but the boat wouldn't be going out until Wednesday. Did he think that after all it would go when the time came, or had they really been stopped as we had heard. He appeared to be very sorry for us and, saying something about his 'god', asked us if we had any money. Kitty told him yes, she had a little, but if we were going to be shut in here for long it would soon go and there was no possible means of getting any now that the mails were stopped. He told her to go at once to the shipping offices and see if there wasn't a boat going, as he thought that one line was running boats to Grimsby for a day or two.

By this time I had found a lady friend who wanted to get back too. She was awfully upset, taking things more to heart than we were, saying that she was quite alone and, Kitty and I alone, we took her along with us to this shipping office the Consul had told us about – it was called the 'Rover'. I might tell you we were afraid to ask a German the way, so we were looking about for a man that looked English. At last we thought we spotted one, but alas he turned out to be a Spaniard and could tell us absolutely nothing, he was a stranger like ourselves. At last in despair our lady friend asked a postman who evidently couldn't understand his own language. Had I myself asked the way I could have forgiven him when he said he didn't understand, but our lady friend spoke German like a native. At last he thought he had struck it, he thought we were looking for the British Consul as every Englishman was doing that day, so he tried to send us there, but, no thanks, we had just left.

While we were still arguing the point with him, a real life German, seeing that we were in sad troubles, came and spoke in good English asking what he could do for us. We soon told him, then he took us into his shop which was quite handy and found the address of the place we wanted. Having got this we thanked him and started off to look for it once more. Our lady friend was all excitement and proved to us a bit of a nuisance, but at the same time a huge joke. Kit and I could have found the place quite easy but that woman – if she asked once, she asked twenty times and it was only five minutes' walk. I shall never forget her and that day no matter how long I live to be.

Well we arrived at this shipping office at last and only to find it packed, hundreds of people buying tickets for England. Our lady friend bought a ticket and was going to sail on Tuesday. She told us there would also be another boat on Wednesday, and tried so hard to persuade us to get tickets to go also, but we told her we had return tickets in another line and we must go there to see if they had a ship going. When we got to the top of the street again she left us and I can speak for us both when I tell you we were mighty pleased to see the end of her.

Now we strolled off to our own shipping office, the 'Great Eastern'. On arriving there we asked when the next ship would be sailing, but he simply said in plain English 'there is no ship you must walk' (needless to say this gentleman was German). The worry of war began to tell on Kit and she asked him if he took her for Jesus Christ, that she could walk on the sea. Here I had a good laugh, and I was not the only one for there was a young English fellow in the office who it greatly amused.

After all the excitement, Rosie and Kitty returned home to their lodgings and shared a simple dinner. This was their first meal at home, as until now they had enjoyed meals in local restaurants, but the diminishing funds at their disposal were beginning to become a problem.

That night we thought things over, we must get back to England is what we were saying, so poor old Kit was counting out her gold to see how much she had and she came to the conclusion that she did not have enough to pay our five fares (our 'Great Eastern' tickets were no use on the 'Rover' line). Once again came forth the great question, what were we going to do? Something must be done. At last Kit said, 'I have plenty of things I could pawn, but I don't know the signs of a pawn shop here. We must find out, so we will ask the landlady'. Well we asked her, and the poor old soul looked at us as though we were things of the past and gave us an address to go to, then we went to bed after a most eventful day, thinking that in the morning we should go to the pawn shop.

Tuesday 4 August dawned – a day that would be remembered as a turning point in history. Germany had declared war on Belgium and immediately commenced an invasion, with the aim of sweeping down into France. Britain mobilised its army and issued an ultimatum to Germany, stating that unless guarantees of Belgian neutrality were received by 11.00pm GMT that evening, war would be declared between Britain and Germany. For Rosie and her sister, however, their immediate concerns were over a much more personal issue. Any worries over the international situation were veiled by sadness over the immediate need to raise money by selling their belongings.

Kit had got out her jewels to pawn and we all had a last look at them. I for one shed a silent tear, for I never thought we should have to do this. Kit reminded me that we had better go to the shipping office first, to make sure that they were still going and we didn't want to pawn our things unless it was absolutely necessary. When we arrived there the office was still full, people were still buying tickets. At last, after being pushed here and there by people half mad with anxiety, we were able to speak with a man over the counter. We asked him if there was a ship running tomorrow, Wednesday, for England. He looked at us as though we were soft, and said something, goodness only knows what, I suppose we frightened him a little. Anyway he called another man to help him. This one informed us that there would be no boat leaving Hamburg on Wednesday and that the last boat for England was leaving in two hours. Kit and I just gave a knowing glance at one another, when the same voice almost frightened us saying, 'You must write to your king, there is nothing else for you to do, perhaps he will help you out of your trouble'. Really I felt I could hit him. Fancy telling us to write to our king, but after my temper had cooled down a bit I took it as a huge joke.

Now we were in the street again. A terrible thing this, no ships to get to England, no work to do, and no money to live on. At least I say no money, we had a little and if we were very careful it would last some time. So now we had to be extra careful, as we were shut in Hamburg and goodness knows how long for. We returned home and told this sad news to the girls, who by this time had begun to take things as a matter of course. There it was – we were shut in and we must make the best of it.

That evening after tea I strolled into the landlady's kitchen and picked up her paper which had just arrived. I looked at it quick, I could not believe my eyes and yet it must be true I thought, yes England had declared war with Germany, at last it had come. How could I go and tell those poor girls this horrible news and yet it must be done. I knew it would be a terrible shock, although we had been waiting for it for two or three days then. As I thought, it was a shock but not quite as bad as I had imagined, they were brave girls. I suppose this was their British pluck. What our feelings were for an hour or so I must leave you to guess. That night none of us slept peacefully. About midnight there was a terrible noise in the street. There was a special paper, what had happened I did not know, but the word 'England' rattled through the street. I thought for sure the war had begun and my heart beat then as it had never beaten before.

To most British people, the German invasion of Belgian neutrality was a clear reason to go to war. The previous day had been a Bank Holiday in Britain, and for many the last such public holiday before Christmas was the usual combination of day trips out and various festivities, although in numerous cases any enjoyment and relaxation was marred by the cries of the news vendors, especially in London, announcing the increasingly bleak political situation in Europe. While there were certainly crowds caught up by patriotic fever in London and the larger towns following the formal declaration of war, far more characteristic was a feeling of quiet uncertainty about the situation. Many felt that the circumstance in which Britain found itself was an inevitable consequence of Germany's political and military manoeuvrings, and that a short war centred around the Balkans, in the manner of the limited fighting in South Africa in which Britain had been involved at the turn of the century, was likely to commence.

On Wednesday [5 August] Kit and I decided to go the Consul's at once and although we both felt that the dear old union jack would be taken down and the British Consul gone we said nothing of it to each other. It was only when we turned the corner by the docks and saw no union jack that we realised that we were alone in the enemy's camp and no one to help us. But it was not so exactly, for in my excitement I ran up those stairs, mindless of the policemen with their rifles who were guarding the place and to my surprise saw a notice on the door, 'Call at the American Consul's' and it had the address underneath. This we copied in haste and off we set once more. After some considerable time we found it, packed with English and Americans as all the other places had been during the last two days. After waiting about an hour the Consul made a speech saying that he had just had a wire from Berlin. The Kaiser wasn't allowing any foreigners to leave the country until the mobilisation was over, which would last about a fortnight. A fortnight, it seemed a lifetime to look forward to, but we could only hope for the best.

The next morning was Thursday 6 August, and the girls revisited the American Consulate to see if there was any news. The first person they saw was the English lady who had bought the ticket to sail for England two days before.

She told us that the boat had been taken up the river only to be brought back by a German cruiser. They were then kept prisoner in the harbour for 36 hours. When we got a little further into the building we saw an English clergyman, and looking a little closer saw with him two young men that looked something like sailors but they had very few clothes on. One had on his engine room outfit which consists of a pair of blue pants and a smock, while the other had just shirt and pants. I felt sorry for these two poor fellows and wondered how they came there like that. But the clergyman told us that they had come into port knowing nothing whatsoever of the war and had run onto the mines and the ship had been blown to pieces. These two by sheer luck had come out uninjured and the majority of their mates lay in the hospital.

Trips to the American Consulate were now a daily occurrence, in the hope that each new day would bring with it the chance of boarding a ship for home.

This morning we saw a lady who enquired how long we had been there, what our business was and what money we had. At this Kit said about £3, then she asked us how much it cost us a day to live so Kit told her, then she thought for a while (I suppose she was counting it up) and said 'Oh, your £3 will last you quite a long time'. We wished the lady good morning and went. When we were outside and quite safe we couldn't help but smile. We had never been asked such questions before, but we had never been to war before either.

Another port of call was the local police station, to which the girls were ordered to report on 7 August. At the sight of five young women armed with their passports, the policemen in the office were dismissive and told them to return the following day, handing them forms to complete so that they could be registered as 'aliens'.

Next day we went the same round, first to the police station and he looked at our papers (which he had given us the day before to fill up) and gave them us back again and told us to come in eight days' time. Then he said, 'When do you intend to leave Germany?' Kit's reply was, 'When you think fit to let us go, we are not staying here for our own pleasure'. Then he said, 'Alright come back in eight days' time if you have not gone'. As a general rule English people get looked on with respect, but just at present it is the reverse and we began to get afraid to go anywhere that the people were not English. Just at present there is only one place where you can find anybody English and that is the American Consul's.

Monday 10 August arrived, exactly a fortnight since the day that the Brewsters had arrived at Hamburg docks and lost their luggage.

What a lot has happened since then. If only we had foretold this, we should not have worried over our luggage being on the ship, but would have simply turned back to join it. Some people would say 'Everything happens for the best', but in this case one would hardly think so. Well on this Monday morning we went down to the Consul's, not a bit lighthearted for by this time we were thinking what a useless trot it was. We were about twenty yards from the office when we met two young men. That they were English anyone could see. As we came nearer one of them spoke: 'There is good news for you today, you are English of course? The Consul has told us to tell any English people we met to be ready, for at any moment they may be able to leave but we have to call round this afternoon when he will be able to tell something more definite.' You can't imagine our surprise, we could hardly believe it. I saw a tear spring to poor old Kit's eyes but it was for joy. I could have done the same but thought I had better not. How delighted the girls were when we told them this good news I must leave you to guess.

In the afternoon we went round as we had been told. There was a young man on the door and he wasn't letting anyone in this afternoon. As we came up he enquired what we wanted. Kit told him she only came to see if there was any news. He said, 'You are English, yes, there is very good news for you. Most likely you will be able to leave in four days, but you must come in the morning.' We were jolly pleased to hear this from the office and returned home with very light hearts.

The next morning came round and off we sailed once more, only to learn that our clergyman had been taken as a spy and stood a very good chance of getting shot. After waiting around there all day we learned nothing regarding our going home, but we heard no end of blood curdling yarns from the other prisoners. One man had come from Berlin on a military train and when eating time came he was asked if he was a soldier. He said 'Yes' and took coffee and rolls with the others.

When we arrived the next morning [Wednesday 12 August] we were informed we must have an American passport. They had evidently got something in their minds, either they were going to smuggle us on the American man of war 'Tennessee' that was coming in a few days to take the Americans away or they were going to try and protect us by saying we were Americans. We had to fill up a big sheet of paper, had to tell even the colour of our eyes, shape of nose and mouth and that was as far as we got that day. That wasn't the passport, we just had to swear to that little lot.

The fourth day [Friday 14 August] had come round. We wondered this morning if we should hear anything definite about going. On arriving at the office our hearts sank, there was a huge notice 'Up till now no possible way for British subjects to leave Germany'. One man tried to cheer us and told us we might be here for years. That day we sold our return tickets so when we do come home, we shall come at the expense of the British government and the sooner it is the better for us, for we are nothing more or less than prisoners. True, we are allowed to walk about the streets, but we are not allowed to speak unless we speak German and as we can't do that we have to say nothing and people look at us as though we have done something terrible. One night a man chased Edie and I with a stick and told everyone else to do the same. I tell you we have never run so fast for a long time. I expect every minute for one of us to be taken for a spy.

Several weeks passed, and August turned into September. Rosie and her friends continued to live frugally, making regular trips to the American Consulate in the hope that an opportunity to reach home would materialise. They were ordered to report every day to the police station; the one day they failed to do so, a summons was received at their lodgings, ensuring continued compliance. The day finally came when the Brewsters' money ran out, but fortunately they were able to claim from the British Relief Fund, drawing 'just sufficient to keep us'. This amounted to five marks or five shillings per day. This was particularly fortunate with regard to their accommodation, as their German landlady had already threatened to throw them out on the street if her rent money was not forthcoming. The fine late summer weather was a welcome addition to their otherwise unfortunate situation, until the American Consulate followed up on its advice to facilitate a return home.

One fine morning we became Americans. Yes it is true, we paid 5/4 for a sheet of paper with a big red seal, we were Americans and nobody could say otherwise, but I never knew until then that one could change their nationality so quickly.

Many times our hopes were raised, and so many times they were crushed. About every ten days there was a notice for ladies to get prepared for the journey, as they might be able to go any moment. When we turned up next morning the notice was turned to the wall.

Their attempts to obtain a sea passage home having failed, the only opportunity that remained appeared to be to try to cross the border between Germany and the Netherlands. Their time spent at the American Consulate meant that Rosie had mixed with many others in a similar situation, and despite their new status as neutral Americans making an eventual return home more likely, the subject of a speedier but covert method of escape was raised.

While down there every morning we met several people who turned out to be fairly good friends, in fact I should say very good friends, two were English doctors and there were three Scotchmen. These people tried their very hardest to help us out, but all in vain. At last we could stand the suspense no longer, so these five men decided to draw lots to see which of them was to take this terrible journey on his own. It was a terrible risk we all knew but something had to be done, if one could get through then we could all go. Well it fell on one of the doctors, Dr P----, it was very sad when we said goodbye to him, for we were pretty sure he would be held up at the frontier and taken prisoner. Days passed and there came no news of him, until at last we heard through the American Consul that he and lots of others had been taken prisoner and were now digging in the fields with a bayonet only a few yards behind. They wrote asking the Consul for money as the prison food was not sufficient to keep them together, as all they had was black bread and coffee. Poor P----, he did that all for us, but we could not help him out.

On Wednesday 23 September, the girls learned that some women travellers were being allowed to pass the frontier, although a certain amount of bribery of the German border police seemed to be required as well as the continued ruse of posing as neutral American travellers. Receiving the money for their travel expenses from the

British Relief Fund, they were finally able to make a start on their attempt to get home.

On Friday afternoon [25 September] we came to collect the money for the journey and told our Scotch friends to get home quickly and write letters, that we could take them to England for them. How pleased those boys were. They were going to get news to their friends at last. This was a great risk, for if those letters were found on us we also should go digging the fields with Dr P----, but our British pluck came forward once more, we were quite prepared to take them – leave it to the Brewsters, they would hide them somewhere. We promised to meet those four boys at six o'clock and collect the letters. When we arrived there, instead of being four, there were about twenty four. They had all told one another. Anyway we didn't mind, the more the merrier, we took them all and only too pleased to do so, and some who had only just discovered we were going brought letters to the station on Saturday morning.

The morning we left, our old landlady shed a few tears. Whether she was really sorry or not I'm sure I can't say myself. I think the money was worrying her, but that mattered little to us now, we were leaving their country and that was all we cared. On arriving at the station we found several friends to see us off, one of our Scotch boys couldn't come as he had sent his boots to be mended. It was jolly hard luck on those boys, they had only come over for a holiday and naturally only had one pair of boots. They couldn't come out when it rained either, as they only had flannel suits and straw hats.

Everything went alright until we arrived at Osnabruck, here we had to change and wait about four hours. While waiting here a convoy of wounded came into the station, poor boys; although they were Germans one couldn't help but feel sorry for them. Some were wounded in the arm, we saw the nurses take them something to drink.

On leaving that station one of our young ladies jumped a flight of stone steps and dislocated her ankle. I really thought the girl had broken her leg and I half carried and half dragged her to the other train which was due out any moment. What my thoughts were perhaps I had better not say, but I can assure you I wished the Germans and the war somewhere. We were very fortunate in arriving at the train in time and after us all telling the girl off for being clumsy, thought it time to look after the foot.

The next stop was the frontier. Here we all began to tremble; looking out at this station one sees nothing but soldiers with fixed bayonets. We got into the custom house and had our hand baggage well looked into. When the custom house officers found no ammunition we were politely handed over to the policemen to whom we had to show our passports. Here we tried our best to hold our tongues and only speak when absolutely necessary in our best American accent we could master (which was very bad).

Kit produced her passport and handed it over. One glance at it and the soldiers with the bayonets were ordered to lock all doors. Here the trembling and cross questioning began. We lived in holy dread of being sent back, or even worse than that, to prison, where we should be made to dig the ground and eat that terrible black bread. Now they wanted to know how five people could travel on one passport, so Kit told them that in America young girls didn't need passports and another thing she was a teacher with her four pupils and if he didn't let her through she would inform President Wilson on her return to America. At this the poor man began to quiver and handed her back the passport, telling her everything was quite alright. We all wanted to shout 'Bravo Kit' but knew we dare not.

The danger wasn't over yet. In order to keep up the charade of being American, their entire luggage had been addressed as destined for New York. An official asked Kitty if she had booked passage on a ship for New York, to which she replied that they planned to catch a suitable boat at Rotterdam. 'You will have difficulty', he said. 'Perhaps you will have to go to England'. 'Oh, I don't want to go to England', Kitty replied. 'I hate the English.'

Before the doors were unlocked, their larger baggage had to be examined, which contained their friends' letters and postcards hidden inside the basket lining. In addition to the fear that the letters would be discovered, the girls were terrified by the fact that their bags also included real swords dating from the South African wars, which the Brewsters used as part of their act.

Eventually the baskets were closed and the boys' letters were safe, those terrible doors unlocked and the soldiers with bayonets ordered to let the American school mistress and her young ladies pass. Oh, what a sigh of relief. 'Success at last.' We who were feeling very sad only five minutes before were now five of the happiest people in the world.

That night we arrived at Rotterdam and were shown great respect and kindness by the Dutch people. Now we could sing to our hearts content the song we had so often thought about but never dared to mention.

'Oh for a rolly polly, Mother used to make; rolly polly treacle duff, rolly polly that's the stuff; only to think about it makes my tummy ache; oh lor lummy, I want my mummy, and the pudding she used to make.'

We left Rotterdam Monday afternoon [28 September] and after a most terribly rough and sick journey under the Dutch flag, arrived in dear old England. You can imagine how pleased we all were after being among the Sausages for so long.

The Brewsters immediately secured a theatrical engagement at Wisbech in Cambridgeshire for a week where, according to Rosie, they 'made up for lost time'.

By this point, the war had begun in earnest, with the first British troops coming into contact with the enemy at the Battle of Mons on 23 August. The subsequent retreat of the British Expeditionary Force came to an end with successes at the Marne and the Aisne, marking the beginning of the entrenchment for both sides which would come to characterise the situation in France and Belgium so strongly for the next four years.

The Five Brewsters on their return from Germany. Kitty is on the far right, with her sister Rosie second from left.

Rosie Neal (1891–1998)

Rosie's only brother was killed at Arras in the latter stages of the First World War. Her sister Katherine Neal, leader of the Brewster Troupe under the stage name of Kitty Brewster, died in 1939 at the age of 60. The last correspondence between Rosie and the Imperial War Museum was dated May 1991, when she was looking forward to her centennial birthday on 30 August. Despite her age Rosie remained active and was a keen gardener in later life. In reference to her experiences at the outbreak of the First World War, she remarked that 'the memory of those days will remain for <u>ever</u>'. She is believed to have died in 1998 at a nursing home in Braintree, Essex, having reached the impressive age of 106.

2 | Hugh

GALLIPOLI
MAY – SEPTEMBER 1915

We could see the line being simply mown down, and it was a very nerve-trying sight

With the opposing armies on the Western Front digging in and a situation of deadlock becoming apparent, the Allies began to look further afield for a means to seize the initiative. German naval blockades and the closure of overland routes had meant that the Dardanelles, a strategically important strait of water leading from the Mediterranean into the Black Sea, had become crucial in order to allow the passage of trade and supplies to and from Russia. This important link between the Russian Empire and its Allies was threatened when the Ottoman Empire entered the war in November 1914 on the side of the Central Powers, as the Turks had ensured that the Dardanelles were made impassable by laying an extensive minefield across the channel. The Russians appealed to their Allies for help in countering the Ottoman threat, while many in Britain believed that action against the Turks would help draw Bulgaria and Greece into the war on the side of the Allies. Both countries had been ruled by the Ottoman Empire and bore a grudge towards their former masters.

A naval attack was proposed by Winston Churchill, the First Lord of the Admiralty, in order to clear a passage through the

Dardanelles and guarantee their control through a small landed force. A minor attempt made in February 1915 was followed by a more determined attack by a larger naval force the following month, but both resulted in failure as the Turkish defences, including most notably the extensive minefield, proved much more effective than expected.

Considerable losses and bad weather resulted in the campaign being abandoned in favour of a ground attack, which would involve an amphibious landing on the Gallipoli Peninsula to the north of the strait. The 78,000-strong Mediterranean Expeditionary Force (MEF) was ordered to land on the Gallipoli beaches, secure the Turkish forts and capture the shore batteries, to ensure safe passage of Allied shipping. British and French battleships could then be sent up the Dardanelles towards Constantinople, thereby directly threatening the Turkish capital.

On 25 April, the MEF landed on six different beaches along the Gallipoli coastline, with the British 29th Division spearheading the attack at Cape Helles, the southernmost tip of the Peninsula. The Australian and New Zealand Army Corps (ANZAC) landed further north, with the intention of cutting off the Turkish forces. The defenders were too few to prevent the landings but succeeded in inflicting heavy casualties, limiting the Allies to a relatively small area of captured ground along the coast. Little was done by the invaders to advance further, and within days a degree of stalemate had already set in.

On their way to bolster the forces present on Gallipoli were several companies of the 1/6th Battalion Manchester Regiment. In command of 'C' Company, consisting of around 200 men, was Hugh Heywood, a young inexperienced officer who, like many of his fellow troops, had not yet served overseas or been under enemy fire. Enlisting in 1914 at the age of 18, Hugh had quickly completed his officer training and by spring of the following year was now a full Lieutenant. For many soldiers, Turkey and the Near

East promised the romance and excitement present in schoolboy tales of the Trojan Wars, and for Hugh the voyage alone was a stimulating novelty.

We spent last Wednesday [5 May] in the Aegean Sea – a beautifully blue sea which was dotted with countless little islands of various sizes; it really was a ripping sight – we were not out of sight of land from day break till quite late on in the day, and each island had different attractions to show us. There were no parades, and I spent the day watching the islands pass by. We passed two quaint 'warships' which didn't seem to have very much to do, but which simply cruised about – I suppose they were patrol boats on watch. On Wednesday/Thursday night I was on watch from 2am to 4am. When I got up I saw the lights of shipping at the entrance to the Dardanelles, but we soon passed these and went on up the coast to Kaba Tepe where the Australians and New Zealanders made a landing.

It got light by about 5.00am and by 6.00 we were all up and watching. There was not much doing – isolated warships and many transports dotted over the surface of the sea, and occasionally we saw the flash or heard the boom of a gun from the hills on shore. Later in the morning we got orders to go back to Cape Helles – which we did. We anchored quite close to a number of battleships (among them the 'Queen Elizabeth', 'Swiftsure' and 'Triumph') and they fired spasmodically most of the day and provided us with good occupation watching their huge shells burst on the western slopes of Achi Baba, raising a huge cloud of smoke, dust and debris. We also detected some of our shore batteries just on the edge of the cliff, and saw enemy shells bursting over them. With glasses, movements of infantry in the distance could be followed, and the whole sight was most interesting, and one not likely to be forgotten for some time.

About 5.00pm on Thursday afternoon a sweeper came alongside and they began to disembark, along with fellow reinforcements from the 1/5th Battalion Manchester Regiment.

We got on to the boat in full pack (very heavy) and [were] taken for a most lengthy cruise all over the place, as if they were uncertain where they wanted us landed. The wind was intensely cold and we shivered huddled together on the slippery decks of the sweeper; our first move was not pleasant. At 9.30pm they landed us on a most ingeniously contrived jetty made out of a series of pontoons lashed one to the other, and all to a large steamer – the 'River Clyde' – which had been run aground there. Our landing was not without excitement; a few shells from a concealed battery on the Asiatic shore plonked into the water quite close to the jetty and one hit a ruined tower near the water's edge, and made a lot of splinters fly.

Once Hugh and his men reached shore, it was soon clear that they had been landed at a location remote from the rest of their battalion. As their boat had conveyed all the battalion's food for the next two days as well as its entrenching tools, the urgency involved in finding the rest of their unit was quite apparent. After some hours of wandering along the only road they could find, the rest of the battalion were finally discovered in bivouacs, asleep, and after dumping their gear Hugh and his men found places to sleep wherever they could. Hugh chose a fairly comfortable place between two piles of biscuit cases, sharing a blanket with another officer as the night was very cold. The heavy firing of the guns meant that any sleep was intermittent. As dawn broke the following day, the light allowed them to take stock of their new location.

There was quite a show going on over the valley in front and great activity at General Headquarters 500 yards away, and we lay in our dugouts or on the grass most of the day just watching and dreaming and expecting an order to shift, and wondering what it would be like when it came.

It is a strange scene. In the distance is a hill – which is the object of all the fuss – and between us and it a big undulating grassy valley with one or two farms on it, and lots of trees. All the outward and visible signs of war are puffs of smoke in the air where the shrapnel burst, lines of newly turned earth which indicate where the trenches are, and stretcher parties bringing in wounded. An aeroplane overhead completes the picture. With glasses you can sometimes distinguish men doubling about near the trenches and groups of men waiting near clumps of trees – just what one has been taught not to do! Close in front and to the right is an open grassy lawn with one or two aeroplanes usually on it; and behind the lawn a low hillock, on the nearside of which the powers that be live in dugouts. I can pick out two batteries of fairly big howitzers, which are firing pretty hard. I expect there are a lot more which I can't see. Behind us is the sea dotted with warships and countless transports. The former shoot at intervals, and when their shells pitch over the distant ridge they cause a huge column of smoke and dust and debris.

As far as we know at present we go up tonight. I am longing to get the first dip over, for waiting is <u>awful</u>. I shan't mind once we've been under fire, but the lack of knowledge as to what it's like disconcerts me rather. I should like to tell you a lot about the ships and the troops and other things, but the censor would certainly object. This is the most interesting experience I have ever had in my life.

The long-expected orders arrived at 7.00pm and half an hour later they fell in and moved off in the dusk, round a hill and along a dusty road, passing on the way several groups of French, Australian, Indian and British troops. The nationalities present on the Peninsula were many and varied, with Indians, Australians and New Zealanders of the British Empire fighting alongside French colonial troops, as well as the Egyptian and Maltese Labour Corps. In addition, the Turkish defenders were commonly led by German officers.

Our men's efforts at French, and the Frenchies' efforts at English, were really very amusing. Some of the Australians were quaintly morbid in their remarks as we passed along, and others were

almost rude – they as much as enquired 'What blankety use these
blankety Terriers could be!' They have really done marvellously
well themselves in conjunction with our 29th Division and the New
Zealanders. The French have not come up to what was expected of
them, but our troops and the Colonials have been simply wonderful
and have achieved marvels in the face of odds which can only be
appreciated when you see the actual places where they had to work
and the things they have to do.

By this time it was quite dark, and the order 'all smoking and
talking to stop' had been passed down after we had gone on a
bit. We turned off to the left along a very twisty marshy path and
eventually they 'fetched us up' not in a sandy desert or in a rocky
patch, but in a real grass field with hedges and trees in them. It really
was lovely – the first field we had been in since leaving England. We
had to dig ourselves in, in readiness for the morning, and on digging
found water at a depth of a foot, which rather upset things. However
we dug about eight inches and piled the earth up in front, then got
more earth from the open space in front to build up the parapet
to the right size. The men had soon got into the earth and were
down asleep, and after gathering some leaves to 'floor' our dugout, I
got down in the middle between Donald and Pilkington and settled
down. And so to sleep.

The extremes of temperature in that part of the world were very
noticeable; nights were especially cold and it did not get warm until
late in the morning. By midday during the summer months it was
extremely hot.

The poor field was no longer a field but a series of lines of dugouts,
the trees and hedges at the sides were still untouched and there were
some ripping wild flowers there – daisies, cornflowers, and a small red
flower. We really were in quite a pleasant spot – near two batteries,
one ours, one of 75s. About noon Brock and Brooke and I went over

and had a look at them in action. The absolute imperturbability of the French gunmen impressed me very much and compared to them our men seemed always in a hurry. While we were coming back a few shells came into the bivouac but they only hit one man.

About 6.30 a most terrific bombardment suddenly started and lasted till 7.30 and as soon as it had stopped an attack was launched simultaneously all along the line. We could only see the part of the line where the French are, and we watched them attack through our glasses – it was awfully interesting. You could follow the whole progress of the fight. First they were behind some clumps of trees in small bodies, then they pushed off in small columns and finally deployed and advanced in rushes, and all the time our guns and the naval guns from right out at sea were simply playing hell with the Turkish trenches – high explosive shell bursting right in the trenches giving a cloud of sickly yellow smoke and a pillar of dust and debris.

The French line still went on and now they were on open grassland you could see their bayonets gleaming in the sun. They got closer and closer to the Turkish trenches and the artillery fire got heavier and heavier, then all of a sudden it stopped and the French got up and swung at the trenches in a thick line, and the Turks got up and ran over the crest of the hill like rabbits and the artillery with lengthened range poured on them and must have done terrible slaughter. The French rushed on past the trench and a hand-to-hand fight ensued which we followed with our glasses; it <u>was</u> a sight, and after a time when things grew quieter, you could see the ground littered with sky blue and brown motionless forms.

It was soon dusk, but the firing did not diminish. Hugh's battalion received orders to fall in and were instructed to advance towards the front line. Progressing over fields until they struck a road leading uphill, they arrived at a bleak common which could be made out only vaguely through the darkness, their surroundings revealed intermittently by star shells and flares fired at intervals by both sides. They proceeded along the road for a while until receiving orders to halt and lie down. There was a small shallow trench to one side of the road, and as many men as possible were crammed into it. Hugh stayed with fellow officer Brock on the road.

While we were waiting and wondering what caused the delay the bullets came pretty thick round us – probably ones fired at the front line trenches rained high – and one of them picked me off in the lower left arm. It felt like a big stone being thrown at me hard – <u>very</u> hard indeed – and I did not think it was a bullet till I felt the warm trickle of blood down my sleeve. Then I got the front man of my platoon, who was lying near me, to get the field dressing from its place in my tunic and he was just going to put it on when Norris turned up going forward and bound me up and put a sling on me and told me to walk back to the base two or three miles away.

Hugh had not been at Gallipoli for two full days, yet had already been wounded. He was no longer fit for front line action and had to follow the procedure for any other walking casualty.

All this happened about 10pm, and I set out much annoyed at having to leave my platoon to my platoon sergeant. The arm hurt a lot at first, but it soon got to a dull throb and I was quite happy, except for the fact that, for the first half mile, bullets were quite frequent visitors and kept on ringing through the air near you or kicking up the dust round your feet.

On my way down to the base I picked up an Australian and a Naval Division man, both wounded, and we went back together. The naval fellow was very bad and nearly dying – he'd got a bullet through the back – and we got him into a cart and didn't see him again. The Australian and I walked on slowly and talked much – or rather he did and I listened – of the glories of Australia and the Australians and so on, which bored me rather, but what took the cake was this: he asked me if I knew London and I said I'd stayed there once or twice and been through it pretty often, and he then asked me if I knew a certain James Williamson who lived in London and was a clerk in a company for the promotion of submarine mining!! I suppose the Australian mind is incapable of conceiving a large town.

They reached the dressing station at 11.30pm and, realising that the medical staff were struggling to cope with an influx of wounded, they pushed on to the base hospital, arriving there soon after midnight.

I was dumped in a big tent and given a stretcher to lie on, and a blanket. This tent was for officers only – there were many others for the men – and it was half full when I arrived and filled up in about an hour which showed that the casualties must have been pretty heavy. There were some beastly cases in it; a man next me had been shot through the stomach and was yelling for morphia, another had got it through the head and was lying still with a blood soaked bandage round his forehead, a third had got it through both cheeks and had got his tongue taken off at the same time, and he was coughing blood all the time and couldn't lie down; and so on. In fact it was quite an eerie place – lit by two poor lamps, with a sleepy orderly sitting by a medical table at one end, and the rows of stretchers all round illuminated just enough to see the white bandages stained a dull red, and not much more – which, in some cases, was rather a blessing. The groans of those badly hit were very nasty at times; in fact that place made one realise, in a very definite way, what a vile thing War is. Death with its sense of peace and rest would not seem half so bad as the spectacle of the hideous battle of Life against Death.

So I got down and tried to go to sleep, feeling rather a cad to have to occupy space there, when there were so many worse than me. About 12.45am a doctor came in; he looked horribly over-worked. He examined all the newcomers and when he got to me he told me that casualties were coming in all the time like flies. He took off my bandage and looked at the arm which was very bruised and swollen, and announced that the bullet was still inside. So he packed me off to 'theatre' – a small tent lit with an acetylene lamp and furnished with a wooden table and some bowls and instruments – to get it taken out. He laid me on this table and washed the arm and then told me to 'get ready' and gave three rapid gashes with a knife whereupon blood poured into a basin conveniently held by an orderly. The doctor then got a pair of sugar tongs – or similar weapons – and dived for the bullet in the gashes he had made. He caught hold of it once and was pulling it out when the grip of the tongs slipped; that was rather uncomfortable. He dived again and this time pulled it out all right, much to my relief. I've kept it as a memento. Then he put in a stick and bandaged it up and the job was over – much to my relief, for it had been very uncomfortable. I went back to bed.

From the position of the entrance hole and the way the bullet was pointing in the arm, and my knowledge of my position when I was hit, the doctor and I came to the conclusion that the shot must have been fired from the right rear, and consequently was due to one of the snipers who are the plague of everyone's existence here. The Turkish snipers are very bold and don't care a penny for their own safety, and they are fiendishly cunning. They work up close to our lines in a most amazing way and conceal themselves and snipe at anyone and everyone. Many of them have been previously concealed before our troops took the country in which they are hidden, and they did much damage at first, and still do a lot, but we are gradually getting to know their ways and how to deal with them. One was in a hole in a clump of bushes with 1,500 rounds of ammunition and food for eight days: he was covered with grass and leaves and his face was painted green! They are up to all sorts of tricks like that and they are a source of great trouble and danger. Besides this the Turks – inspired by Germans of course – are full of all manner of ruses such as wearing our uniforms, shouting wrong orders in English (with a faultless accent), sending wrong messages, and so on.

Hugh remained in his bed throughout the night, although any sleep was likely to have been interrupted due to his arm wound throbbing and the necessity of having to lie on his right side. Morning dawned to reveal the news that two officers in the tent had died during the night, while a swift chorus of Turkish shells resulted in Hugh fleeing for shelter into a convenient nearby trench until the worst had passed.

About midday we were moved off in a lengthy mournful procession to the beach where there was a lighter with a pinnace under a very youthful Middy. This took us off first to a sweeper, which in its turn conveyed us to the 'Braemer Castle'. The boat filled up completely with wounded on Sunday evening. There are about 40 officers on board but only 25 get up and, of this 25, half hobble about. We are mostly Australians and New Zealanders and there is one RMLI, two RND and one Lancashire Fusilier besides myself to make up the English contingent. There are 940 men on board, five of the 6th Battalion, and there are some awful cases.

We spent Monday [10 May] lazily, reading and sleeping; as far as we could tell it was quiet on shore. It is awful being so close and not knowing what your friends are doing or how they are getting on. We sailed in the evening for Alexandria – it is strange to have such a speedy return to the old place again, and since then the life has been one dream of eating and sleeping and reading which would be very nice if it wasn't for the thought of the others left behind there.

The hospital ship *Braemer Castle* conveyed its wounded soldiers to Malta, stopping off at Alexandria en route in order to refuel. The doctors on board continued to work on their patients, removing bullets and dressing wounds throughout the days and nights; numerous casualties died during the voyage. Despite the discomfort of his wound and the disappointment he felt at having left the Peninsula so prematurely, Hugh made the most of his time on the ship by playing bridge with fellow officers. They arrived at Alexandria

harbour at midday on Thursday 13 May. Those patients fit enough
to disembark were able to explore the Egyptian port and buy much-
needed supplies. Hugh was still wearing the uniform in which he
had been wounded, sporting a ripped sleeve, and did not even have
a toothbrush to call his own. After enjoying a treat of strawberries
and cream at a local café, they sailed again the following afternoon
and sighted Malta around midday on Monday 17 May.

*We were lowered in a sort of box into an old barge which was towed
by a tug to a smaller landing stage further up the harbour. Here we
found a strange crowd; an officious old DADMS in all his finery, some
Maltese police, many ladies armed with cigarettes (of the vilest sort),
biscuits, lemonade, flowers, etc. and, doing noble work, some Maltese
boy scouts (mostly getting in the way), and lastly some ripping people
who lent and drove their cars to convey us [to the hospital]. Outside the
barriers there was a crowd of the populace and whenever a stretcher
case was put into an ambulance a little pious gasp went up from the
onlookers. In the end we all got packed into cars and they pushed us
off to [St Andrews Hospital] – driving at a most breakneck speed.
When we got here they gave us tea and then sent us to bed. While
we were having tea, Field Marshal Lord Methuen (the Governor)
came up and asked us if there was anything we wanted. He is an old
man, bow-legged, with about four yards of ribbons on his breast and
I thought it was jolly decent of him to trouble to come. The beds here
have springs and sheets and they gave us pyjamas. It really was very
nice. The pyjamas are War Office issue of strange cut and immense
size, and they nearly fall off even when you tie and button them up as
tight as possible! Still they are very nice. And then to bed, to sleep and
sleep, better than we had ever slept for a long time.*

While the novelty of a decent bed, food other than bully beef and
biscuits and the lack of military routine were an obvious boon to
Hugh, it did not take long for him to realise that hospitalisation on

Malta was far from the most rewarding experience. His arm wound began to heal, but his muscles remained stiff and any exertions resulted in pain and discomfort. Frustration at being away from the fighting began to become increasingly evident in his letters home.

20 May: Up late as usual, and another morning spent as lazily as before. In the afternoon some of us got into a vilely rickety kind of cab and drove down to the ferry to go across to Valetta, where we wanted to do some shopping. We had tea at a moderately English cafe and then went to the club and read papers. A 'Sphere' I saw there had a birds-eye pictorial map of the Dardanelles, and it really was the most inaccurate thing I've seen for a long time. They put mountains where there are plains, and got the whole thing about as wrong as it could be. I wonder who amuse themselves drawing such things.

21 May: This morning I have been trying to write letters but some Australians have been playing the gramophone continuously for about one and a half hours and it has rather got on my nerves! The Australians here are a strange crowd – very trying to be with for any length of time, some very decent, and others as uneducated and unmannerly as it is possible to imagine.

23 May: Our life here is terribly monotonous – in the morning we are lazy and get up as late as we can so long as we are in time to get a bit of breakfast. After lunch – the morning is spent in utter laziness – we may go down town and have tea, and do any necessary shopping, and then we come back here to a most deplorably awful dinner, after which a game of cards or a book serves to pass the time till bed claims our attention once more. Of external news we get none – rumours of the intervention of Greece and Italy, and statements from irresponsible individuals that utterly impossible things have happened in the Dardanelles.

However, things would eventually improve. Saturday 19 June brought the news that an order had come through for Hugh and several others to embark on the transport ship *Euripedes* that afternoon. Initially presuming that they were destined to return to Gallipoli, he was amazed to learn that the ship was in fact sailing for England. It all seemed too good to be true.

Their ship entered Plymouth harbour in the early morning of Sunday 27 June, and within days Hugh had reported before a medical board which declared him fit for active service. His short recuperative leave would be spent at his parents' home at Alderley in Gloucestershire, to which he was returning for the first time in almost 11 months. But the period of rest was not to last, and the journey back to Gallipoli began the following Sunday, with the transport ship *Kalyan* leaving port at 5.00am.

We saw Plymouth go and become a blur, and then saw England gradually vanish in the distance; it was a grand sight but a sad one, and our thoughts were strangely mixed. One doesn't realise when one has not been out of England what a wonderful place it is. Most of us were up watching and we watched in silence till even the one with the keenest hope and the most vivid imagination could not say he saw any more.

Their ship arrived at the island base of Lemnos on 19 July, and orders were received to report that evening to Gallipoli's 'W' Beach. At 6.40pm they cast off and had an uneventful four-hour voyage across to Cape Helles, although Hugh and his comrades were not allowed ashore that night and so endeavoured to sleep in huddled crowds on the deck, sharing bully beef and biscuits through the cold and discomfort. At 5.00am the next morning they landed, and after reporting to the beach commandant, Hugh set off to try to locate his regiment.

The change to the landscape since he had last been there was quite noticeable; the green countryside with grass, trees, hedges and wild flowers had now become brown and dusty, scarred with trenches, dugouts and shell holes. A conspicuous feature was a large wired-in cemetery with many graves, each with its own wooden cross. After much wandering, he arrived at the headquarters of his Infantry Brigade, the 127th, and was then directed on to the support trenches where his men were currently located.

I sought the part of the trench where C Company are, and put my gear in the dugout which I was going to share with Milne and Kershaw. It consists of a recess in the forward side of the trench wall raised three inches above the level of the floor of the trench; it is about 14 feet long, 4 feet wide and 6 high to the top of the parapet, and when it is sunny we spread ground sheets over the top and sit hunched up inside. You can make yourself quite comfortable, once you get used to your surroundings. The rest of the day was spent either reading or eating meals; these your servant cooks for you, and if he is smart he can make a lot of nice dishes with the material available. I had to have a new man – my old one having been wounded – and at present he is not expert, and very dirty. I am hoping he will develop soon.

After a smoke in the moonlight we all dossed down and slept soundly. I was up as officer on watch from 11 to 12, and then slept soundly again till 3.00am Saturday, when we were all roused for the morning 'stand to arms' an hour before dawn. The firing during the night is rather heavier than during the day, but that really isn't saying much. The Turk apparently does not aim his rifle, but shoves it over the parapet and lets fly; at any rate a lot of bullets whistle over, a few hit the parados and fewer still the parapet in front. Pretty well none of them hit anybody, and the average casualty rate at present for our battalion in these trenches is ¾ of a man a day!!

Shells occasionally arrive here, but most of them sail over the trenches. One has just burst on the parapet near here and knocked four men down. When they picked themselves up – unhurt – the only remark made was by one man who asked 'Where's my damned fag!' The only really annoying part of the life is the continual firing somewhere. Either our guns or their guns never let ten minutes go by without a shot at something, and every few seconds there is the whiz-ping of a bullet somewhere near. Otherwise life is all right, but rather dull – in these trenches at any rate.

Hugh had expected his return to life in the trenches to be accompanied by positive action in some way, but his recommencement of active service was rather a disappointment. Just over a week after his return he declared that:

Our existence here has been more monotonous than anything I have ever endured before. We have been stuck in the same place in the same trenches doing the same thing – nothing! Those people who have been here all along say that they have never had a more dull time during the whole time they have been here.

However, things were about to change. The evening of Sunday 1 August saw Hugh and his Company move closer to the enemy, as they were ordered to take over a section of trench in the front line. An inspection of the area had already revealed that the dead body of a fellow officer could be seen quite near but out of reach in no man's land, along with half of his platoon; nobody had been able to retrieve the bodies to bury them. The days were now exceptionally hot, and the ubiquitous dust and flies made life very wearisome. Water, supplied to the troops with a large percentage of chloride of lime in it, was far from ideal for quenching one's thirst.

During the night in the firing line there is one officer per company on watch. He is awake and responsible for the front of his company and he has to walk up and down and visit the sentries, and see they all know their duties and keep a good look out over the parapet. He has to rouse the company if anything in the nature of an attack is made, and he is provided with a pistol which shoots white flares, which he can use if it is too dark to see any particular object. Really, the responsibility for the whole company and the safety of a good many more rests with the officer on duty. I was on from 11 till midnight, and nothing happened during that time. We easily heard the Turks digging in front, but it was too dark to see anything. I organised several bursts of fire just to show them we were awake too: five men firing two rounds rapid all at the same time produce infinitely more moral effect than if they all fired five rounds independently.

Two days later, Hugh received a piece of news which boosted his morale considerably. He had been ordered to take over command of the battalion's machine gun section, as the previous incumbent of the role had been invalided to Alexandria.

So now at last I have got the job I longed for. In addition to the intense interest I have in machine gun work, the job has certain other advantages, and one disadvantage – that you are separated from the battalion most of the time, for the M.G. Section is under the direction of the Brigadier through the Brigade Machine Gun Officer and is independent to the battalion. This disadvantage is in some ways an advantage – because it gives you a delightful feeling of independence and you are responsible to yourself for all matters connected with the section. Normally, also, you have slightly more scope in your choice of dwelling place than the average company officer, because your guns are usually not all together and you have to choose a position which is conveniently near all of them.

After three months on the Peninsula, it had become evident that the Allies had failed to make significant progress in their attempt to capture Gallipoli. A new offensive was planned for the beginning of August which would see a twin-pronged attack punching out from Anzac Cove towards the heights of Sari Bair, while two fresh divisions of infantry landed at Suvla, the large bay to the north. Hugh's machine gun company would play an important role in a diversionary attack at Helles, planned for the night of Friday 6

August. The day before was therefore spent moving their guns to the new position, about a quarter of a mile away.

Moving is always a hard job because one goes about with so much bulk ammunition; we had to cart the three guns and tripods (about 60 lbs each) and 45,000 rounds (about a ton and a half) of bulk ammunition, three spare part boxes and other oddments, in addition to the men's personal kits and arms and ammunition. We had to cart all this stuff quarter of a mile; dig gun emplacements, and mount the guns, and it took us – we were 40 all told – from 9 till 4 to get all the work done. Of course we all had to take up new abodes, and the only place I could find, so as to be close enough to my guns, was actually in one gun position itself in a very small traverse with two NCOs and two men. There is an infernal squash and one can't lie down properly; there is no shade to be had anywhere, the dust and the flies are too awful for anything, and the smell from the corpses rotting in front of the parapet is indescribable. In fact it is quite the nastiest trench I have yet been into.

On Friday we roused early and spent the morning in giving our guns a final overhaul, for we knew they would soon be very severely tried. As it turned out we did not have to use them that day. At about 1.00pm the Turks started a heavy bombardment of our second line trenches; most of the shells went just over the trench we were in, but a few came in but did no damage to us except to make the parapet fly about. This bombardment came as rather a surprise, for we intended attacking and consequently did not expect a bombardment until our preliminary bombardment had started.

At 2.00pm our own bombardment started, and I've never seen or heard or smelt anything like it. The shells were bursting wherever you looked, there was a hellish din, and over all a dense cloud of pungent sickly yellow smoke, through which nothing could be seen distinctly. Bits of shell were flying about in every direction, either from Turkish shells or from the 'blow-back' from ours, which, in the case of some of the bigger ones, was immensely powerful. This went on for nearly two hours, and then they calculated that by this time the Turkish trenches would be smashed, and the Turks themselves either killed, wounded or gone. So they ordered a charge, and all the line from the sea on the left to the Krithia Nullah got over the parapet and went for the Turks. But the artillery calculations had calculated wrong for once and the Turks were there in bigger force than had been dreamt of and as soon as our fellows got over, an absolutely hellish rifle and machine gun fire was opened on them. They fairly dropped, and it was a vile sight; but the dust soon got too thick for us to see further than 30 or 40 yards from the trench, so that we who had had to stay behind could only listen and hope.

After a time one or two wounded began to crawl in from in front. One poor fellow crept back very slowly under a heavy fire and rolled fainting into our arms over the parapet. When we came to dress him we found he had three huge holes in his stomach, and half his inside was outside. We did him up as best we could – it took five field dressings to do it – and I morphined him and sent him back on a stretcher.

This went on all the evening, and when night came I am sorry to say we were hardly any further on than at first, and the fighting in front was – as far as we could judge from reports received – just as desperate. The idea of the whole operation was not so much to gain ground – though this of course was desired – as to draw the enemy's attention from the new landing at Suvla Bay which was made at the same time. As a feint it was eminently successful – but very costly.

Meanwhile the main attack at Anzac had stalled and, in a manner not dissimilar to the initial April operations, the Suvla landings would see little ground seized other than that adjacent to the beaches. On the morning of 7 August, Hugh's machine-gunners crouched in their trench waiting for the preliminary bombardment for the second day's attack to cease. Their job was to target any Turks who might be sent up in support.

At intervals I was able to direct our fire through the smoke from the bursting shells, and it seemed to be going to quite the right place. In the half hour the three guns got through about 6,000 rounds, so I hope we did some damage. I had a lucky escape; a bit of shell hit me on the cheek and the blood fairly poured for a bit but it was not serious and soon dried up. One of my corporals got a broken finger, and was rendered useless, and another got a slight wound in the arm; and two guns were temporarily put out of action by bullets but we managed to get them going again. Those were all the accidents that we had, so we got off very luckily.

At 9.40 the line charged, and got a dreadful time from shrapnel and the enemy's machine gun and rifle fire. We could see the line being simply mown down, and it was a very nerve-trying sight. Being so far away from the battalion we did not know at the time who had gone over and who were left, but afterwards I learnt that out of thirteen officers who went over the parapet nine were killed, two were wounded and two came back unhurt; out of 200 men who charged there are about 100 left. Hunter, Reiss and Milne all got done in and the rest of the killed are fairly new people. Kershaw got wounded in the back and knee – so I was told – and escaped being killed. The left of our battalion must have got into a machine gun, I think. You can pick out at least 30 bodies lying in a space of 20 yards square – one of them is Milne and he is on the parapet of the Turkish trench firing down into it with his revolver. Later in the day a shell burst over them, and four of them got on fire and only their charred bones are left. I'm afraid there isn't much chance of getting Milne's body in. Fighting went on all day, and in the end we found we had got one trench that we had not got before: an expensive feint!

Sunday was far from a day of rest, but one of vigilance accompanied by the constant heat and flies. There was desultory fighting but no change in their position. The following morning Heywood's

machine gun section estimated that their two guns had killed or
wounded about 80 Turks in under an hour.

*It was a great sight, seeing them roll down as they came up the
trench and they didn't seem to realise that they could be enfiladed,
or to know in what direction our fire was coming from. I think we
quite helped the fellows in our advanced trench on the other side
of the nullah. Later on we heard some of our wounded – who must
have been out there since Saturday afternoon – calling for water
but we can't get at them, for it is not allowed to send a party out in
daylight. It would be quite impossible to get to them.*

*The fighting went on during the day, and there was no change in
the position. I hope we are relieved soon; when we are I shall sleep
and sleep and sleep; at present I am very tired. The constant shelling
and rifle fire, the constant sense of responsibility, the lack of rest (for
the last five nights I've averaged three hours sleep per night, and that
sitting, and in full equipment), the heat and dust and the flies of the
day, the uncleanness of one's life (I've not had my trousers off for a
fortnight or a wash for six days) and last, but not least, the awful
casualties and the sight of all the dead, dying and wounded, have all
continued to make me feel quite incapable of doing anything but the
mechanical work which has to be done each day.*

As the offensive slowed and petered out through August, Hugh
and his machine-gunners were moved out of the front line in order
to enjoy the relative calm of the support trenches. Even so, the
immediate threat of danger remained, albeit from unlikely quarters.

*During the morning my exasperation at the filth and squalour of
the trench and of myself got hold of me, and since things were very
quiet I handed over control to my sergeant and went down into the
gulley 200 yards away and had a most excellent wash all over in
a small bucket of evil-smelling green water drawn from a sluggish*

stream nearby, higher up which two long-dead Turks were peacefully reposing. I was away about an hour and a half, and on my return, after donning clean socks and shirt for the first time for ages, I felt a new man.

Coming back up one of the communication trenches I came upon two men cleaning their rifles, and one of them was just putting back his bolt and thoughtlessly shoved it home without examining the breech, then pulled the trigger. Of course the magazine was charged and the gun went off and the bullet passed right through the other man's neck, and he fell, spouting blood at my feet. The man who shot him promptly got hysterical so we bandaged the poor fellow up and sent for stretcher bearers, but he died before they turned up. The man who had shot him went quite mad – for he was his best friend and wrote his letters home and read those he received to him, for he (the mad man) was incapable of doing either – and had to be forcibly restrained from hurting himself. It was not a very pretty incident. A little later on two men were digging a little higher up the trench, and one of them hit the other on the head with a pick and killed him. I think we have enough casualties without ugly incidents like these.

The August offensive had failed to bring the decisive victory which had been hoped for, and the usual routine of trench skirmishes resumed. Shells and bullets were not the only danger faced by soldiers, however, as the unsanitary conditions experienced by those fighting at Gallipoli meant that a significant number of troops were evacuated with sickness such as typhoid, diarrhoea and dysentery. Hugh had been fortunate enough to hold off the worst of such symptoms, but by the beginning of September he had begun to experience a lack of energy and frequent bouts of illness, which led him to report sick to his Medical Officer.

He sent me on to the Field Ambulance who looked at me and labelled me 'catarrhal jaundice' and gave me instructions to present myself

at the jetty with my kit at 4.30 to catch the evening lighter off to the
hospital ship. And in this way I was invalided off after seven weeks
on the Peninsula.

For Hugh, the Gallipoli campaign was over – but for others it would continue until the end of the year, when a mass evacuation was ordered following winter storms which lashed the Peninsula. The campaign had proved to be a failure due to the effectiveness of the Turkish defence, while a good deal of public criticism back in Britain highlighted the political and military failures of the operation. By the autumn of 1915 the focus for many had returned to the Western Front, where a potential breakthrough was being championed by the French High Command.

Hugh Heywood (1896–1987)

Following his experiences at Gallipoli, Hugh was transferred to the Indian Army in 1917 and served with the 74th Punjabis, remaining in India where he took on the duties of a staff captain. Marrying in 1920, he had a son and a daughter. On his return to England in 1923, Hugh secured a first in Theology from Cambridge and was ordained at Ely in 1926. Returning to Cambridge as a Fellow and Dean he found himself in great demand as a university preacher. In 1945 he was invited to become provost of Southwell in Nottinghamshire, where he remained until 1969. As the Very Reverend Hugh Heywood he embarked on an unusual programme designed to enliven the Cathedral community, which included welcoming dogs to the minster and encouraging miners to sing 'Roll Out the Barrel' at a service. Latterly, he ran the country parish of Upton in Nottinghamshire and died in 1987, aged 90.

3 | Eric

THE BATTLE OF LOOS
SEPTEMBER – OCTOBER 1915

I left our trenches at the head of my company and set out into the night on my way to the unknown

The opportunity to serve one's country as a 'weekend soldier' appealed to many men in the years running up to the First World War, and the formation of a Territorial Force in April 1908 was designed to create a home defence army ready to mobilise for this purpose when needed. Any member of the force could additionally volunteer for overseas service, and among those keen to 'do their bit' was Eric Gore-Browne.

Educated at Malvern College boarding school before attending Worcester College, Oxford, Eric had been called to the bar at the Inner Temple in 1909. He was married in 1912 to Mary Booth, daughter of the famous philanthropist and social recorder Charles Booth, and in the same year joined the London Regiment as part of the Territorials. Over the next couple of years, Eric worked his way up as a junior officer. By the time of his arrival in France in March 1915 he was 29 years old and had risen to the rank of Captain. By autumn he was in command of a Company of just over 200 men in the 1/8th Battalion.

Eric's arrival in France coincided with serious discussions being held between the British and French high commands to seek a means of returning to a war of movement in France and Belgium. By the end of 1914, trenches had been dug from the Belgian coast to the Swiss border, with the opposing armies facing each other in a deadlock characterised by frequent shelling, sniping and skirmishes, both sides searching for the chance of a breakthrough. This situation persisted throughout 1915 while the British concentrated much of their effort on the campaign to force the Dardanelles and capture Gallipoli.

The plan put forward to break the deadlock by the French Commander-in-Chief, Marshal Joseph Joffre, comprised a series of attacks along the Western Front which were designed to exploit the numerical advantage which the Allies enjoyed over the Germans. The French would spearhead offensives in the Champagne and Artois regions, while the British would lead a smaller, more northerly attack at Loos. Lord Kitchener, the British Secretary of State for War, supported Joffre's plan as it was felt that a successful attack would draw attention away from the struggling Gallipoli campaign and take pressure off the Russians on the Eastern Front, where the Germans were concentrating their efforts in 1915.

Field Marshal Sir John French, the British Commander-in-Chief, was rather more cautious, pointing out that the landscape around the town of Loos was utterly unsuitable for an offensive since the coal mining town was surrounded by slagheaps (*crassiers*) and colliery towers. As these towers and high ground were currently occupied by the Germans, this would mean that any British attack would be overlooked by the enemy, putting the attackers at a distinct disadvantage. The ground itself was also a problem, being predominantly chalk and so presenting clear difficulties when digging defensive trenches. One consolation, however, was that the Loos offensive would see the first British use of a secret weapon which, it was hoped, would cause enough casualties and chaos to swing the balance in the attackers' favour.

This desire to break through the German line and escape the monotony of trench life would have been shared by Eric and those men under his command in the 1/8th Battalion London Regiment. Known as the Post Office Rifles, due to the high number of post

Eric Gore-Browne, in a photograph believed to have been taken in 1914

office employees among their number, the battalion of volunteers was part of the 47th Division chosen to lead the initial British assault towards Loos, which was scheduled for the early morning of Saturday 25 September 1915.

The night before the attack saw Eric and his men in a state of nervous anticipation. As they readied themselves at their billets in the nearby village of Noeux Les Mines, Captain Gore-Browne was fully mindful of the plan for battle and his own Company's part in it, which at least initially would be as reserve troops.

We go up tonight. I am the first company to move as I have the furthest to go, but am the back company in anything we have to do and, anyhow, that can be very little I think. Our job will be sitting tight with clenched teeth and I know I can rely on the men which is a very great comfort to me now.

However, an unexpected development had arisen at the last moment.

Rather a blow has fallen. This morning a new order came round worded like this: 'Owing to the number of officers which a Battalion may take having been reduced, the following officers will not proceed with their companies tonight – 2/Lt Maitin and 2/Lt Bounin'. So at the last moment when all my arrangements had been made and all my officers thoroughly instructed and reconnoitred, I am bereft of two of them. Ten altogether have been taken from us, all these new men. Did you ever hear such madness? However there it is and I must make the best of it and I shall have Smith and Gardiner and the other platoons under sergeants whom I know I can trust. But it is vexing.

I am getting much more philosophical the longer I am a soldier, and we shall pull through somehow, but they don't make it easier for us. Maitin had tears in his eyes when I told him he was not to come – poor boy, it is very hard on him. He has worked hard on our line and knows it backwards and his men like him. He is a great loss to me. The order to reduce came from high authority and the Commanding Officer whom I dashed off to see can do nothing to help. But did you ever hear such a thing? The day the Battalion moves into possible action, ten officers are to be left behind. Ye Gods! – I should like to have five minutes with the man who is responsible and give him a bit of my mind.

That evening the Company began to advance towards the front line. Although their journey was only four miles, the traffic congestion caused by the movement of other troops and supplies in preparation for the battle meant that it actually took nine hours to reach their start position, which was in the support line trenches below the village of North Maroc.

It was an awful journey – we were not allowed to move by the roads for fear of shelling, and the trenches were narrow and uneven, and no lights allowed. We made the whole air sulphurous with our views on war generally. Finally we got there very weary, and the trenches we occupied were too full to allow rest, even if we had felt like it. Luckily we were not shelled much during the night. I made coffee for all I could on my little stove – for sure the most useful thing I have, and a rum ration was served out to those who liked it.

Eric's Company of the 8th Londons were part of the 140th Brigade. In front of them, in the firing line trenches, were the 6th and 7th Battalions of the London Regiment who were to form the spearhead of the attack while, stationed in readiness in the houses of North Maroc behind them, were the 15th Battalion.

Where we were at Maroc was the turning point, or right flank of the whole movement. Loos was about half a mile on our left. Our Division was ordered to take the two lines of German trenches and then form the right of the southern defensive flank of the British force. We had to move forward about 1,200 yards and swing round right handed and dig ourselves in. I think it was a fairly important job.

The feature of the German line to our immediate front was the Double Crassier – two huge slack heaps thrown up by a mine at their eastern end. These were about 50 feet high, and ran parallel east and west and the German front line ran round the western end or nearest edge to us. The two were about 700 yards long with a path in between, and look more like two fingers than anything. Our objective included the clearing of the Double Crassier. In the event of the attack being successful we were to link up our old line with the German front line.

Early on the Saturday morning, the offensive began. The secret weapon used by the British to precede the assault was poisonous chlorine gas, which had first been utilised in a widespread way by the Germans in the Second Battle of Ypres five months earlier. While the British had responded with outrage to this new un-gentlemanly weapon, a short time only had passed before they decided to adopt the method themselves and Loos would be the first such opportunity. Over 5,000 cylinders had been transported secretly to the front line trenches containing gas ready to be released and directed towards the German trenches just prior to the British infantry going over the top. The high level of secrecy surrounding the use of the new chemical weapon was still evident when Eric recounted the event some days later, requiring him to make only a guarded reference in his letter home.

The attack was timed to start at 5.40 and punctually at that hour our initial steps were taken, which I may not tell you about yet, but I do not think they helped us much. At 5.50 the Germans, who must I think have been fully aware of what was coming, opened a tremendous fire upon us. Rifles, guns and shells of all kinds seemed to pour down all this time, our guns were going 'all out' too and the noise was awful. I sat in the trench feeling very frightened and occasionally took trips along my company to pass the time of day. They were all cheery and we had only about six casualties here, wonderful luck considering the amount of shells there were coming. The other companies who were on my right got off even easier.

At 6.20 the whole line in front of us got up and over and went straight for the German line – I shall never forget the sight – from my line I saw the Scots to my left going straight line after line to Loos, in front of me the 6th and 7th in four waves of men went straight for their objective, the Double Crassier, and the ground to the left of it. The smoke hung everywhere and I was too busy with my own show to watch for more than a moment, and wish 'God speed' to them with a very sincere lump in my throat.

The gas released by the British drifted slowly over the German lines where it proved to be moderately successful, taking the enemy by surprise and causing the intended confusion among them. Further north towards La Bassée, however, the wind direction meant that the gas was blown back towards the British attackers, making its application far less effective. As support for the main offensive against Loos, Eric and his men waited in their trenches for news of how successful the first attack had been.

The shelling we in support got was perfect hell – I think it was the worst half hour I've ever had – but again God looked after us. I never expected to get through – my company lost five killed and seventeen wounded here, all by high explosive shell.

Immediately, I had word that the 6th and 7th were clear. My orders were to move down to the new support line and occupy the whole of it. This went all right, although there was some confusion owing to the dead and wounded in the communication trenches. It seemed a lifetime waiting there, but good news came very soon, and the first we heard of possible success was about 120 prisoners who passed us in the smoke on their way back under escort, all taken in the first German line by the 6th and 7th. Such fine men they were.

At about 8.30 we heard the attack was successful and the 6th and 7th had reached the German second line and we were in telephonic communication with them. Immediately the Brigadier moved up three companies of ours to support and be there in case of counter attack, and I only was left. Our three companies got over safely – only about 20 casualties, and the position seemed fairly secured.

The 47th Division had gained all their objectives that day, but at a cost. Nick Lloyd, in his book *Loos 1915*, recounts how 60 officers and 1,352 other ranks were casualties in this first phase of the attack. Much ground had been won, however, and the British had successfully occupied a considerable section of the German front line trenches.

Eric and his men waited for further orders beneath the continuous enemy shelling. A priority request was suddenly received from Maxwell, an officer who had gone over with the first three companies, who needed urgent reinforcements in the way of bombers and grenades. Eric sent forward six boxes, each containing 30 grenades, and all ten of his company bombers.

It appears that the Germans counter-attacked about 3pm with bombs down the southern side of the Crassier. The Germans came down and our fellows had blocked the trench there with sandbags and earth and held all the trenches north of that point. Thomas went over with my ten men and I hear he was splendid. I had news soon that we had stopped the attack and would I send my reserve machine-gunners to man a German machine gun that the 7th had taken and which they wanted to use to cover any further attack down the southern side of the Crassier. I got them together and off they went. I did bless the day when the British army began to concentrate on specialists. This battle has shown that we cannot have too many machine-gunners or bombers. I kept up a stream of bombs to the other side and finally about 5pm got the word 'to send no more for pity's sake!'

By this time we had good news from the left that Loos was taken and many prisoners and wounded came through us, both German and English. By this time the rain was pouring down and I had lost my hurricane smock in the early stages and was soon very wet.

It got dark soon after six and I was beginning to think that I was not to have a show at all, when the order came from the Brigadier that I was to move out, over, and occupy the southern Crassier and form a defensive flank to the rest of our Brigade. I was left carte blanche how to do it, and about 7pm I left our trenches at the head of my company and set out into the night on my way to the unknown. I cannot describe that walk to you. It will be a dreadful memory for ever. I went right through the battlefield with all its dreadful relics – it was my nearest touch to war, though I had had men killed and wounded by me in the early stages – but on this walk, I went right through it all; the profusion of dead and wounded makes one's heart stand still. We got over safely, a machine gun to our right had a go at us, but shot too high, and I reached the old Hun front line without a casualty. There I found Maxwell and had a little talk with him, and made my dispositions.

I took one platoon up between the two Crassiers and at the eastern end made them climb up the southern slopes and lie down. Four men were actually on the top looking down on the Huns, and the rest lying just a little way down on our side of the crest. I felt that the four men would be quite enough to look out, while they would be able to summon the rest and line the top in case any attack developed. My other platoons I disposed in a similar way, keeping one in hand at the western end in case of trouble.

It was very exciting work, putting out the company in that awful place – imagine a pouring wet night, on a slack heap, or rather two slack heaps, full of shell holes and German wire, dark as blazes, and every possibility of running into the Huns at any moment. We fell about and got blacker and blacker, and the rain by this time had permeated every stitch of my clothing. I was very relieved when I had got them all out and I made my headquarters at the western end, in an old shell hole, and prayed like St Paul for the dawn. I visited my groups from time to time, but bar occasional shots over our heads, and one or two big shells that hurt no one, they did not worry us at all. I think the Hun had had a pretty good shaking.

Dawn broke on Sunday 26 September and shortly before 5.00am Eric received word that he was to withdraw his Company from the Crassier and move forward to occupy part of the recently captured trenches which had been the old German front line.

I moved there, getting into position about 5.30am. By this time it was getting light on Sunday morning and I got my men spread out, and sentries posted, and set out to explore the German trench. They are wonderful soldiers. This trench had been bombarded by high explosives for five days and it was practically unhurt, only the dugout blown in. Most of these are at least 17 feet deep, and quite impregnable. The trench itself was floored throughout with fascines and revetted and showed signs of deliberate and skilful carpentry. Everything was neatly labelled – directions, limits of sectors, officer dugouts, etc. all clearly marked. They had left in a great hurry and there were helmets, ammunition, rifles, haversacks, food, beer bottles, equipment, letters, papers, boots and every conceivable thing strewn about. I found a lot of explosive bullets and kept a clip as a trophy – also a beautiful telescopic rifle which I have brought away with me.

I visited all the dugouts and rounded up about five slightly wounded Huns, fine big men, all very frightened, and they seemed surprised when I got their wounds dressed and gave them water. 'Good Camarad, no punish' was their stock remark; but I am afraid we none of us left much sympathy. I sent them back to our line under escort; two being carried on our stretchers.

By this time it was 8.00am and Eric and his men enjoyed a breakfast of tinned bully beef and biscuits. He lamented the lack of his stove, which had been left behind with his pack. A fellow officer, Guy Portman, suggested reconnoitring the ground over which they had just advanced, that had until recently been designated no man's land. Setting out accompanied by two stretcher bearers, they thoroughly searched the ground over which the advance had taken place and found countless wounded and dying soldiers.

There were a very great many for whom we could do nothing, but I like to think that two or three may have owed their lives to us. Guy was quite splendid. The shortage of stretcher bearers was quite awful, and those we had worked like heroes, but we could not get nearly enough and we were not able to get all we wanted away till late on Sunday night, and the attack was in the early hours of Saturday morning. This was nobody's fault. The RAMC were heroes, every one of them. There were not many German dead, about 30 in my company sector. I think most of them must have gone to their deep dugouts, and when our men reached their trenches, those men gave themselves up and ran for it. The Brigade took about 250 prisoners all together – all fine men, well equipped, and I could see no reason why they ever let us in, for their trench was practically intact, and they had heaps of ammunition and on each fire step piles of hand grenades ready to throw. About 12 o'clock Guy and I stopped, both done to the world; and we drank a bottle of beer between us. While we had been working out on the top, the Huns had not worried us much. Their third line – we had taken their first two – was about 1,000 yards from us and bar an occasional shot and one dose of machine gun, they let us attend to the wounded unmolested, for which I take my hat off to them.

During this time, except for those who had been left on sentry duty, the majority of the Company had been able to get a certain amount of sleep, albeit disturbed. As soon as Eric returned from his excursion, they set to work to consolidate the captured German trench and make fire steps facing the appropriate way. While undertaking this work, the Company were in a position to witness the reserve troops of the XI Corps being sent into a renewed attack which launched at 11.00am.

From my dugout in the German trench I could see our Royal Horse Artillery batteries galloping up the Lens Road into position behind Loos, and the most wonderful sight of my life – the Guards moving over open country, under a curtain of Hun shrapnel. They marched as if in Hyde Park, and I was very, very proud to think that they were some of them friends of mine.

At 7pm I got orders to again move my company to occupy the Double Crassier. We had had no food except what we had brought with us on Friday night and we were fairly miserable physically. I made the same disposition as before, and the night passed away sleeplessly. The only incident five inquisitive Huns whom we met on the South Crassier, but who ran on seeing us... we stayed up there longer on this Sunday night and were not withdrawn until 5am, well nigh frozen, as the cold on the top of our wetness and fatigue made things pretty rotten for us. However by this time, good things were beginning to arrive from behind and rum and hot tea came up about 7am on Monday morning – which made new men of us.

That morning saw a significant German counter attack to the left of Eric's position, and any uncertainty shared with his men about the course of the battle was exacerbated by stragglers retiring from the front line with news of further British casualties. The reserve troops, who had seemingly arrived too late to consolidate the positions already captured on the 25th, had had to face uncut wire while suffering from a lack of covering smoke or gas in their advance against strengthened German positions.

Unaware of the disappointing outcome of the fighting in front of their position, Eric's men continued to work feverishly in their captured German trench, which had now become part of the new British support line. Removing and burying both British and German dead was one of the unpleasant necessities, but their morale remained buoyant.

The capture of Loos was a magnificent achievement carried out with a dash and utter disregard of danger that made the spectator very proud of being an Englishman, and now we have got it I don't think we shall lose it again in a hurry and its twin towers that have a view of the whole country for miles around are a possession well worth having. They are really the winding gears of a big coal mine but for some reason are of immense height and are made of steel girders. There were originally three side-by-side but our howitzers blew one down and the other two have resisted all efforts on our part for the last six months.

I was very glad when Monday night came and I got news I was not to occupy the Double Crassier again that night and that No 2 were to have a turn down there. I got a few hours sleep and we officers Smith, Gardiner and Penny shared the night between us, our first sleep since the Thursday before. I occupied the dugout of a German subaltern, beautifully made and full of his belongings – there were several boxes of cigars which the men enjoyed and many pairs of boots and vests and drawers which also came in handy. I was too wet to sleep well during my three hours off. The wind having gone round to the north, the cold was quite horrible.

On Tuesday afternoon, Eric took his Company further forward in order to relieve the 7th Battalion London Regiment who were holding the front line. By then his Company numbered about 87 men and, with only another 40 available from another company, it meant that they would be holding the line very thinly indeed. But, as Eric put it, 'there was nothing for it', and at 2.30pm they started off up the old German communication trench on the north side of the Crassier.

I got there safely with the first two platoons but then the relief was spotted and the Huns shelled us heavily with the result that from about 3 till nightfall (6.30pm) I was left in the front line with two platoons while the remainder of my little force lay dogged in the line behind me waiting to get up as soon as the shelling ceased. It was a dreadful afternoon, pouring cold rain and water over one's ankles in the trenches. There was not a single dugout in the line I was to occupy and nothing for it but to sit in a puddle and twiddle one's thumbs waiting. At last the rest of my little force arrived and we got into position and let out the 7th Battalion – poor fellows, they were very much shaken and done. After their attack on Saturday morning till this Tuesday afternoon they had no shelter or relief, with the constant possibility of a counter-attack hanging over them, and it was good to see their pleasure at departing. They lost pretty heavily, officers especially.

There was a good deal of work to do in this line and neither sandbags nor tools were easily procurable – my fellows worked like good 'uns, all night and all day, Tuesday night and Wednesday night and Thursday and raining heartily all the time and we put in about a thousand sandbags and changed the whole complexion of the trench. This line had been a German support line and intended merely to hold supports and not to be held as a defensive line, and it was little more than a deep ditch.

There was only one point in front of us which gave us any anxiety. The Huns had constructed a machine gun emplacement which played on us when we worked by daylight and they had also put loophole places for snipers there who continually worried us. They were not good shots but we all of us had some near shaves. On Wednesday at midday I sent a report to the Brigade about this and in a very few minutes came back the message 'Please observe and report for artillery'. The point was only about 150 yards in front of us so you can imagine it was quite exciting hearing the shells coming and whumping into the ground just in front of us. The fifth was a direct hit and we were no more troubled.

I was very proud of the way my little command worked, every man realised the importance of making the new trench as strong as we could and as quickly as possible, and night and day they kept it up. When not working, men had to be on sentry as we never knew when the Huns might try and get their own back again. My little show was nearly 1,000 yards from my nearest supports and even these were fully occupied in looking after the Crassier and the blocked trench on the southern side and could not have helped me much. It was very exciting and I had no time to feel tired.

The unrelenting freezing rain led to a general feeling of discomfort, the men being wet through and having no shelter in the way of dugouts. The British reserves had been used up and the French Army therefore began to take over the Loos sector, freeing up the exhausted 47th Division.

On Thursday night relief came in the shape of a French Colonial regiment. A little lieutenant with a very strong company of stalwart

French men took over about 9pm still in pouring rain and my weary mud-stained lot ploughed their way slowly out, done to the wide world, most of us with five days beard and feeling as if we had never known what it was to sleep. It was a pitch dark night and we came back across the open from the western nose of the Crassier. The new communication trench was blocked by incoming Frenchmen. To Maroc and thence a very slow and weary march to some ruined houses behind our trenches at Philosophe. We were in some sort of reserve here for the night. The filth and desolation of these houses passed everything, they were full of bits of equipment, bully beef, rifles, and the hundred and one things that get thrown about in a battle and the house I was in had no doors or windows. We found a mattress and Smith was asleep within ten minutes of getting there. I made some coffee and Penny and I found a mattress and clasped literally in each other's arms we soon fell asleep, waking up occasionally to curse the cold. Wetness seemed nothing compared with the cold.

The march back to more substantial billets began the following morning, with the promise of a well-earned rest away from the trenches. The respite from the immediate danger of shelling and sniping allowed Eric to reflect on his experiences of battle and the effect of the last six days of being under constant fire.

I walked round and saw a little of the battlefield in front of this place before we left. No painting or poem or writing will ever give you a picture of a battlefield either while it is actually on or afterwards. I am glad to have seen both. There is something very magnificent and unselfish about it and death in many shapes and forms, some beautiful, some ugly, makes one feel less fearful about it all and that there must be a hereafter where all these brave good fellows are going to meet again and have their reward. The last week has been a whole lifetime full of wonderful things and sights which I shall never forget and which no words of mine will be able to describe adequately. I am more tired than ever before in my life, and the luxury of a bed in my nice billet here, last night, was one of the most wonderful things I ever knew. I think things are going on well, but the job is not nearly finished yet and it is extremely hard out here to get a comprehensive view of the whole thing and not let the success of one's own little bit make one too sanguine. All the time the battle was on I kept on thinking to myself how I could write about it and what I could tell.

I think the French have really had a huge success, but of our own I am not so sanguine. I know nothing of the Champagne country but if you can realise what it is to attack a series of Whitwicks and Thringstones [small Leicestershire villages near where his wife had grown up] you have our problem in a nutshell.

Despite the initial successes of the British advance on 25 September, the failure to consolidate their new positions meant that while some ground had been captured it had been at a significant cost in lives. A concerted effort was made by the Germans to recapture the lost terrain by launching an offensive along the entire front line around Loos, but by the evening of Friday 8 October this was abandoned following heavy casualties. The British planned a final attempt to advance further by capturing the tactically important Fosse 8, a dominant slagheap, on the following Wednesday. In this, Eric's Company would play a crucial part.

At 2am on Wednesday morning, just as I was light asleep, came the order to move and away we went again to some trenches more to the north so as to be directly in front of Hulloch and just behind the 46th Division which was to make the attack of the 13th. We did not get into this new position till dawn was breaking – in fact we were lucky to get to ground before daylight. If we had not, I shudder to think of the consequences as we were on the top of a ridge in full view of the Huns. However all went well and we lay doggo till 12 noon when the bombardment started. It is impossible to describe it. It was more severe than that of the 25th as every gun in the neighbourhood was concentrated on a front of not more than two miles and I should not like to estimate the number of shells that went over us. It was Hell let loose.

At 1 o'clock the gas and smoke started from our lines – an awful scene – a layer of smoke and below it the greens and yellows and purples of the gas and in the midst of it all the bursts of shells of every bore. I've seen two of these gas attacks now, they are indescribably awful – hell could not be worse. After an hour of this, at 2pm the assault started. I could see it all from our immediate front. Away up to the north the Hohenzollern Redoubt and Fosse 8, and in front of us Hulloch and, to the south, Loos. The assault was lost in the smoke and we could see or hear nothing of it during that long afternoon when the Germans gave it us pretty hot as they always do to supports and we had every kind of shell on us. However we were very lucky – only a few casualties.

About 7pm came the order for us to move forward and rumours that the attack in front had not been able to hold its gains. We heard there was to be another try in the night and we were wanted to help it in case of need. However the Division in front of us was too done to have another try and though we moved about 12 midnight into the German trenches we captured on the 25th we were not called on to attack. I wish we had been. We always seem to make the same mistake – supports are not rushed in quick enough and so disaster.

The following day was spent lying in their old German trench, waiting for orders. At 2.00pm Eric was told that his and another Company were to go up and relieve the 1st Queen's Own Cameron Highlanders in the front line. He set out to reconnoitre.

We had a look at the bit we were to take over – very beastly it was. The poor Camerons were very shaken, this awful bombardment and then an attack over the open with its ultimate failure and you can imagine the result of this on their nerves. Added to all they had been a week in the trenches and they gave me a horrible account of the bit I was to have. I went back very dispirited and about 6pm on Thursday I led my company down the uncomfortable communication trench.

My troubles soon began – I found we were on a salient with the Germans practically behind us on two sides so that we got continuous sniping from both rear on two sides and also the front. The trench was in the line we took on 25th September and was in very bad repair and quite unsafe in parts and of course no dugouts. About 5am they began to throw trench mortars at us – the second landed right in the trench and killed two and wounded two. The third wounded four more but the rest they sent, about a dozen altogether, did no damage except morale. They throw a 56 lb shell which makes a frightful noise. The only trench mortar we had was out of action owing to lack of ammunition and the wire to my supporting artillery was for the moment broken by shells. I think that was one of the worst early mornings I ever spent. That was Friday. The day passed quietly, we sniped one Hun and had three or four wounded by shells. Saturday at 6am, again came the trench mortars and killed one more of my men and wounded two others – incidentally buried me and my breakfast in chalk. At night I could not sleep as we were so close to the Hun and on such a salient into his line that all our wits were wanted.

Further bombing on Sunday morning caused additional consternation among Eric and his men but they were lucky enough to avoid any further casualties. Snipers, however, remained an inherent danger in this part of the line.

Poor Gardiner was killed this morning by a sniper. He had been very rash and was out over our parapet in the mist of the early morning burying a dead Scotsman. He was killed quite instantaneously. On Sunday night after a good deal more of this beastly sniping we were moved back to trenches which are about 1,000 yards behind the line. It was a very dreadful time, the worst I've had and the men and officers were very done and jumpy.

Following the failure of the British attack on 13 October, the Battle of Loos was officially over. The heavy rain which continued throughout October, combined with the sustained shelling by the German defenders, meant that any further offensive in this sector would not be a feasible proposition and both sides therefore dug in for the winter. Plans began to be made for the following spring, and many hoped that 1916 might finally bring the much sought-for breakthrough which Loos had failed to achieve.

Eric Gore-Browne (1885–1964)

Eric served throughout the rest of the First World War in various staff posts and rose to the rank of Brevet Major, being decorated with the Croix de Guerre and Distinguished Service Order. After demobilisation in 1919, he joined the merchant bank of Glyn, Mills & Co, starting as secretary but soon becoming a partner and, ultimately, director. In tandem with his business interests, Eric followed a distinguished career as a Territorial soldier, commanding the Leicestershire Yeomanry during the 1930s and retiring from service, rather reluctantly, in 1941. Following the outbreak of the Second World War, he served in several senior Quartermaster General roles and acted as Controller of Rubber, an important government post designed to administer a vital resource which was scarce during wartime. Giving up Chairmanship of Glyn, Mills & Co in March 1944, Eric was appointed chairman of Southern Railways until nationalisation of the service in 1948, received a knighthood the same year, and was appointed as High Sheriff of Rutland in 1957. A prominent churchman and supporter of charities, Eric remained an active director of Glyn, Mills & Co until his death in 1964, at the age of 78.

4 | Herbert

CAPTIVITY AND ESCAPE
NOVEMBER 1915 – APRIL 1916

We were now on our own with few provisions, no compass of any kind, and only a sketchy and far from accurate map

'As everyone knows', remarked Herbert Ward soon after his training as a pilot with the Royal Flying Corps, 'there is nothing intrinsically difficult about taking an aeroplane into the air, but returning it safely to earth has always been something of an art'. Herbert's experiences during the war would see him prove the truth of this adage.

As a two year-old child, Herbert had moved with his parents to France at the turn of the twentieth century, where the family bought a rambling converted farmhouse overlooking the Seine valley. His father worked as a sculptor in Paris and filled his studio with African weapons and shields, souvenirs of the five years he had spent as an explorer in the Congo. Following the outbreak of war in 1914, the family were forced to retreat to England. Once the Germans had been turned away from Paris, however, Herbert's father began to arrange for the conversion of their French home into a Red Cross hospital. Herbert himself was keen to do his bit, and chose the Royal Flying Corps as his service of choice. The RFC was the newest and, to many, most exciting arm of the British Army, having been set up in 1912 for the purpose of undertaking reconnaissance duties and guiding artillery fire. The involvement of aircraft in war remained relatively novel, with their true potential as technological innovations still to be fully realised.

Herbert was commissioned into the RFC in June 1915, aged just 17, shortly after his first successful solo flight on 26 May. He continued training in the BE2, the British two-seat, single-engine bi-plane in common usage throughout the war, and in July 1915 received a posting to No. 16 Squadron RFC based in France. The next few months were occupied by reconnaissance missions over the German lines with only occasional bursts of anti-aircraft fire to distract him from his observation duties. Such missions usually involved taking photographs of the enemy's territory for subsequent analysis, and relied on rather primitive technology.

Aerial photography was something which kept the Pilot very fully occupied, for he had not only to manoeuvre his machine over precisely the right map square, but needed to insert each fresh plate into his externally mounted camera at an angle which would prevent it from being snatched out of his hand by the force of the slipstream.

While on such a mission with Digby as gunner, we encountered an Albatros armed with an immensely long machine gun which immediately fired at us. Our Lewis gun was no match for this sort of thing, since it had to be shifted from one side of the cockpit to the other, by which time our opponent was well out of range. We sighted him again soon afterwards, however, and this time in an ideal position. Digby opened fire, but after the first half-dozen rounds our gun jammed (the cartridge guide spring having broken). Our potential victim, unaware of his advantage, fortunately decided to make for home. This may well seem to have been a fairly harmless encounter, but our team-mate, similarly engaged in photography that morning, did not escape so lightly. A 'streamer' [i.e. message] dropped by the Germans over our lines a few days later contained the news that 'Leutnant Gay', the pilot, had died of wounds and been buried with full military honours, while 'Oberleutnant Leeson' was now a prisoner of war. No. 16 Squadron had hitherto been very lucky, for these were its first two casualties.

The officers had been shot down on 10 October by the German air ace Oberleutnant Max Immelmann, and their loss would prove an omen of things to come for Herbert. Tuesday 30 November saw him acting as Orderly Officer in the Squadron office, on telephone duty – never, as he later remarked, a very popular job. The telephone rang and he scribbled down the message from Wing Headquarters, asking for additional photography of some enemy defences.

The area was one that I happened to know rather well; the weather was cloudless, and I was given permission to go. While concentrating on the camera's needs I had my attention drawn by Buckley (the Duty Observer who had been delegated as my gunner) to an Albatros a little way above us and apparently not aware of our presence. The pilot must have caught sight of us as he turned, for we were then given a perfect view of his black-coated observer operating a machine gun of the same sinister type as had been directed at us on a previous occasion. Firing short bursts as we circled about one another, we soon ran out of ammunition, so there was no alternative but to make for home. Our opponent evidently had the same intention, for he turned away as though he regarded the duel as having been honourably settled – or so we thought. Just then a blood-curdling shriek came from our engine, and it stopped dead. A lucky shot from the departing Albatros had pierced its underbelly, and the whole thing had seized up solid.

The four blades of our propeller, normally invisible, now stood out starkly motionless like the sails of a disused windmill. Since we were almost 6,000 feet up and only a short distance behind the German lines, our predicament did not seem unduly serious, but the wind had meanwhile been rising, and we were making but little headway as we steadily lost height. It soon became clear that, even by diving towards our own lines, we might – or might not – be lucky enough to flop down just inside them. During this time our conspicuously spread-eagled propeller betrayed our helplessness, and we were a sitting target for the German infantry in their trenches, their rifle and machine gun fire being only too clearly audible without the comforting sound of an engine to disguise it.

Small arms fire from the German soldiers in the trenches below them was slowly but surely proving accurate.

Part of a wing-strut and other portions of our machine were now disappearing, the rattle of firing from below increased, and it seemed as though we should inevitably be shot to pieces. Yet to turn away deliberately and land on the German side of the lines was unthinkable, although by carrying on as we were we could hardly hope to get beyond no man's land. Buckley looked round inquiringly, and I nodded in a way that was intended to be reassuring.

Suddenly Herbert himself was hit.

I felt an intensely sharp burning pain in my left leg, in response to which my right foot spasmodically gave the rudder-bar a jab that sent the machine into a turn and thereby lost us our remaining height. Some sort of earthworks loomed up ahead as we skimmed crab-fashion over a trench full of soldiers. Buckley was now wisely climbing out of his seat, and I saw him jump clear as the machine hit the ground. In a scrunch of splitting wood I was somersaulted forward and pinned upside-down, as the after end of the fuselage folded over on to itself like a scorpion's tail.

German soldiers came running up and stood there gaping at the wreck while I shouted and cursed at being left in my capsized position, with my legs in danger of being crushed by the swaying fuselage. Buckley, now held captive between two soldiers, called out that he was sorry not to be able to help, and I saw him being led away. The tail of my poor No. 1717 was eventually lassoed and hauled back, leaving me the right way up, with a compulsive desire to stay where I was and go to sleep. Efficient hands nevertheless lifted me out, and I was taken into a communication trench on a stretcher.

Immensely fortunate for having been able to handle his aircraft despite the complete engine failure, Herbert had negotiated the barrage of German bullets and survived the impact of the crash, only to become a prisoner of war. In a manner perhaps typical of the gentlemanly conduct expected from officers of both sides, he handed round his cigarette case in a gesture evidently welcomed by his captors, who treated their new prisoner with respect.

Exploding shells now began to come over from the British side (for the crowd of Germans that had gathered round the wreckage must have offered a tempting target for our gunners), so I was not sorry when our stretcher party reached the comparative safety of a Field Dressing Station. While the Doctor was examining my wound I looked the other way, imagining the leg to be so mangled and gory as to be fit only for amputation. However, when he had finished some painful probing, to see whether a bullet was still lodged in the knee itself, he tidied everything up and left me with an Interpreter who asked me to hand over all my possessions. He then asked whether I would like to send a message back to the Squadron. Remembering what had been done in the case of Gay and Leeson, I was only too glad to write a short note. Was there anything else I wanted? Yes, there was: I would very much like to meet the airmen who had brought me down. The Interpreter seemed doubtful about this, but promised to make inquiries.

The hospital was based in Lomme, a small town to the west of Lille. As the ward was filled with badly wounded Germans, Herbert soon felt rather conspicuous dressed in his khaki shirt, lacking any real knowledge of the German language.

The note hastily scribbled by Herbert Ward
after his capture, which was subsequently
dropped over British lines by the Germans

*Later on that day two German officers in resplendent uniforms
[Oberleutnant Yilling and Oberleutnant Kraft of the Munich Flying
Corps] were ushered into the ward and directed towards my bed.
Clicking their heels and saluting simultaneously, they introduced
themselves, and in hesitant French expressed their regret at having
brought me down. We then shook hands, and in the course of a
short but very friendly conversation they presented me with signed
photographs of themselves and showed me some snapshots of their
new machine. After another handshake and a further salute they
moved towards the door. I called their attention to some parcels
which they had left behind, but with a dismissive gesture they
disappeared. The parcels contained a bottle of Grand Marnier
liqueur, a hundred cigarettes, and a carton of chocolate eclairs. None
of these gifts appealed to me just then, as I was feverish, but the*

doctor was delighted with the Grand Marnier, the orderlies were grateful for the cigarettes, and the nurses appreciated the eclairs.

Soon the Interpreter appeared in order to return Herbert's pocket book and other possessions, his French money having been scrupulously changed into German currency.

He mentioned that the British had been shelling Lomme during the past few weeks, but had not hit the building in which we then were. I naturally retorted that the British were not in the habit of shelling hospitals. 'Ach so', said he, 'then they know that this is a hospital?' 'Yes, of course', I answered, for I vaguely remembered hearing someone mention in the Mess that there was a building in Lomme with a Red Cross painted on the roof. Even so, I felt guilty of having been indiscreet. On the following afternoon I was transferred to Lille, and the Lomme hospital staff came to the door to see me off, with much waving of hands and handkerchiefs as the horse-drawn ambulance moved slowly away. It was all very touching. Three days later the Interpreter appeared again, shaking with indignation. He announced in furious tones that the hospital at Lomme had just been shelled to pieces: doctors, nurses, patients – all had perished. I could find nothing to say. It was, of course, possible for the building to have concealed a military headquarters on the upper floor, but this idea only occurred to me some time after he had left. In any case I regarded it as a calamity, and could only hope that it was due to some mistake.

The hospital at Lille was a large building but at that time accommodated only about 30 or 40 patients, all German soldiers apart from Herbert and Captain Darley, a fellow RFC officer formerly of the Indian Army. Darley had been hit in the hand by a piece of shrapnel, and the wound had become gangrenous; his thumb had already been amputated, and his fingers were now permanently crooked. The unmistakable stench of gangrene pervaded the fortress-like room that the two British officers shared. The chief surgeon was Dr Custodis who, along with the nursing staff, treated the British prisoners with both consideration and skill. The patients were brought three day-old copies of *The Times* and *Daily Mail* to read, and could send for an orderly to obtain small luxuries from the town.

The German Doctor was a frequent visitor, and spoke good English, but he had a provocative way of insisting that England had entered the war on the wrong side. He would also declare that Germany had much to teach the British about how to govern India, airily dismissing Darley's first-hand experience as irrelevant. His arrogance would indeed have been insufferable, had he not been so essentially good-hearted. My damaged knee interested him, since it was unusual for a bullet to have passed right through the joint without having either severed an artery or damaged the bones. The wound itself remained unaffected by Darley's gangrene, and I was soon able to shuffle about with the aid of a crutch, being passed fit for travel shortly before Christmas.

The sight of someone in khaki uniform being driven through the streets in an open cart was a sufficiently unusual event for the people of Lille to be moved to mild, but promptly suppressed, cheers. On arrival at the railway station, which was teeming with German troops, I spent the next hour sitting on a bench, heavily guarded, and being stared at by weary-eyed soldiers in field grey.

Herbert's destination was Valenciennes, some 20 miles south-east of Lille, where he arrived on 23 December.

At a place hitherto known to me only from a height of 10,000 feet as the final objective of our Long Reconnaissance, I was put into a ward of the local hospital which had been reserved for non-Germans, and now contained a mixed bag of civilians of all ages, a few French soldiers, and a sizeable group of unfortunate Russians who had been wounded while being forced to dig trenches for their enemies. On one side of me was a mentally deranged Moroccan, and on the other a British Staff Officer whose left arm had been amputated at the shoulder. He told me that there had been a desperate shortage of anaesthetics at the time of his operation, and that he had become fully conscious while the surgeon was busily at work with the saw. One of his legs was badly shattered, and had no fewer than eight draining-tubes dangling from it.

Captain Rose had been wounded in the first days of the Battle of Loos and explained to Herbert that conditions in the hospital at that time were appalling, the hospital staff having been completely overwhelmed by the sudden and apparently never-ending flood of British casualties. Other survivors from Loos had been gradually transferred, until he alone remained. Herbert's arrival at Valenciennes coincided with his eighteenth birthday, but he decided to keep this information to himself since he was keen to be seen as older (and more worldly wise) than his true age.

The Moroccan on my other side was convinced that he was due to be murdered. Sitting up in bed and rocking himself backwards and forwards he kept repeating, 'On va me tuer! On va me tuer! Je vais mourir!' ['They're going to kill me! They're going to kill me! I'm going to die!'], until I found myself wishing that his fears would prove justified. In the bed beyond him was an old soldier whose injured lungs made him pant like an exhausted dog, all day and all night. At the far end of the ward were the ragged and heavily bandaged Russians. As an admirer of Tolstoy and Dostoevsky (though without knowing a word of Russian), I hobbled across towards them and tried to establish friendly relations, but they seemed so bewildered that I soon gave up the attempt.

Christmas festivities continued despite the war.

Some French Sisters of Mercy came round the ward, distributing parcels with a kind word for everyone, and I received a pair of braces. On Christmas Eve the Germans arranged for each of us to be given a present (mine was a cherished 'Koh-i-Noor' pencil), together with a Christmas card and a glass of 'champagne' which was greeted with derision by the French contingent.

I was then informed that I was to leave that same evening, together with the Russians. During the 20-hour journey to Cologne I was guarded in solitary state, as the only officer in the party, by a gruff old member of the Landwehr whose curious ornamental pipe, constantly refilled with rank tobacco, was almost as lethal a weapon as his antiquated rifle. On arrival at Cologne, we were all taken in an ambulance to Festungs Lazarette. Here there was one room for officers; three beds, two of which were occupied by French officers. We had bedsteads and spring mattresses. The room was very comfortable and well heated. The senior of the two French officers with whom I shared a room was a grizzled veteran, a Capitaine who disliked everything British on principle and made no secret of the fact that he particularly despised flying men, whom he described as swollen-headed shirkers. His hostility was something which I had never previously met in a Frenchman, and I had no adequate defences. The junior officer, also a Capitaine, belonged to a different generation and did what he could to reduce the tension, but without much success.

The event which impressed Herbert most during his stay at Cologne was the Christmas service of the Russian Orthodox Church, which was held in the hospital chapel on 7 January 1916.

The attendance was larger than I had expected, and I felt rather self-conscious as the only non-Russian present, but from the moment when the prisoner-choir's first deep-toned chord acknowledged the priest's greeting, I found it all so satisfying that I soon lost all sense of time and place. In spite of not being able to understand a word of the service, I felt entirely at ease with these wounded Russians: we seemed to have entered another dimension.

Herbert's recovery from his crash had kept pace with the convalescence of his French room-mates in the hospital at Cologne, and the three of them were soon marked for transfer to the nearest prisoner of war camp.

The senior Capitaine's knowledge of German, hitherto an unsatisfactory qualification since it caused him to be influenced by what he read in the German press, proved useful during the journey, for he made such a favourable impression on our escort that we almost ceased to be aware of captivity as the train chugged slowly along the picturesque banks of the Rhine. We were abruptly reminded of it, however, on being led through the clanking gate-house of the Citadel at Mainz, and then locked up in a dismal room with heavily barred windows. Through these windows we were nevertheless able to watch our fellow prisoners next morning when they assembled from all sides for the 'Appel', and subsequently strolled in pairs and small groups round the Barrack Square. There were representatives of all the Allied armies: Russians in their long porridge-coloured greatcoats, Belgians in black cloaks and caps resembling tasselled tea-cosies, French in a variety of uniforms, and British in khaki, with an occasional brown leather flying-coat.

Before long I noticed that one of these coats was somehow different from the others: it had a fur collar and a familiar look. Its wearer did not come close enough for positive identification, but I felt certain that it must be Duncan Grinnell-Milne, and so it proved to be. An untimely engine failure was responsible for his having landed on the wrong side during a Long Reconnaissance, but he was determined to bring his captivity to an end at the earliest possible moment – no waiting for the war to be over by next Christmas or any nonsense of that sort. He was housed in one of the more modern of the three 'Abteilungs', along with a handful of other RFC men whose one idea in life was to organise an escape. This made them unpopular with some of the more senior British officers, the Regulars who had been captured during the Retreat from Mons and Le Cateau, whose training had taught them to regard capture by the enemy as one of the legitimate hazards of war.

ded an undue interest in escape as a selfish activity which damage the general well-being. Such were the two schools t in several camps. Since I could still only walk with the aid , the possibility of escape had never crossed my mind.

The camp consisted of three separate buildings, forming three sides of a 400 yards square, surrounded by two rows of barbed wire. Two of the buildings were new and contained about 200 men each, with an average of eight in a room. The colonels had rooms to themselves, all of which were well ventilated, while the other officers shared in twos. The third building, however, in which Herbert was held, was very old and formed part of the citadel of Mainz. The tunnel-vaulted rooms were dark and dirty, with an average of 12 or men to each, with beds sometimes placed one above the other.

g RFC wings, and having upper bunk,

little t ally about 1½ hours tnight. What little there at all. The streets of Main abitants we saw were inv esmen's carts, no horses, t 9.30am we paraded in fro

days solitary confinement.

In Herbert's building there were no facilities for washing except basins in the room, while the latrines were 'disgraceful and insanitary'. They were allowed a warm shower once a week and a cold one every morning.

The food was bad; we got the following. Early morning: coffee, which was bad – not like coffee. At midday, we went to a separate dining room and had for the most part sausages, quite uneatable, and fair soup, it might have had meat in it. About six inches of black bread for the day. The next meal was supper, at 7pm in the same building, consisting of much the same as lunch, with beer and wine extra. There was a canteen, open three days a week only fro[*m*] *8am to 12pm and again from 3pm to 4.30pm. Jam was the* [*...*] *food obtainable, prices rather expensive; smoking materi*[*...*] *certain articles of clothing could be got. Cooking was* [*...*] *our living rooms and so we formed a kind of mess and lived almost entirely on the contents of our parcels, which we cooked on small spirit stoves obtained from the canteen. Bread arrived regularly for us in good condition from the Red Cross at Berne. Any tinned food was kept in a cellar, and could only be opened in the presence of a German sergeant.*

For exercise, we could walk about the square and we started some hockey and tennis – the net was not allowed to be string, but wire. A week or two before I left, they started walks in the town and the country round. We were in parties [*...*] *nationalities, under the gua*[*...*] *we had to w*[*...*] *gene*[*...*] *fo*[*...*] *us* [*...*] *inh*[*...*] *tra*[*...*]*

a sergeant. When the numbers were checked, an officer passed down the line and we had to salute. At 4.30pm, the same again. At 8pm we were again counted in our rooms and a guard sometimes came round about midnight. Punishments consisted of solitary confinement in a cell; this was not very terrible as you could have books and food and a good bed.

Perhaps due to the large number of French prisoners, who began to arrive on a regular basis after the opening of the Battle of Verdun on 21 February, Herbert and three other British officers transferred to a new camp on the evening of Saturday 4 March. Escorted to a second-class train carriage, they travelled south through the night to Vöhrenbach, a prisoner of war camp for officers located 3,000 feet up in the Black Forest region.

It was a pleasantly snow-covered village whose inhabitants seemed a cheerful lot compared with the townsfolk at Mainz and Cologne. A hundred or so French officers were already installed in the handsome new school building, with only four British and five or six Russians. The tall thin Commandant was a surprisingly benign figure for a Prussian Colonel, and our central-heated surroundings could hardly have been more attractive. He impressed upon us that it was the best camp in Germany, and it certainly was very good. The food was better cooked and served than at Mainz; the bread was better though made of sawdust and potatoes. Jam, sardines, sweets and fruit, besides articles of clothing, on sale at the canteen.

The discipline was the same as at Mainz only the roll calls were at 10.30am and 9.30pm. You had to be present at lunch and dinner, where you were counted. There was a cell but it was not required; all were contented and well-behaved. My pay was 60 marks a month, from which 54 marks were deducted for meals, whether eaten or not. The grounds in all could not have been more than 100 square yards, which was decidedly insufficient for exercise; for recreation indoors we had a piano and two billiard tables. Smoking was allowed anywhere. Hot shower baths could be had three times a week and cold every day.

The two senior British officers, Major Godman and Captain Binney, were both in very poor health and hoped to be invalided to Switzerland, but the remaining five of us were prepared to take life light-heartedly, Newbould giving mock salutes and cheeky greetings to the stout Canteen Feldwebel, and all of us 'covering off' during Appels in such a way as to falsify the numbers.

The approach of spring encouraged the local population to take its Sunday afternoon stroll along the road that went past the prison camp. The inmates, who one might have expected to be made to feel like animals in a zoo, rather took the opportunity to turn the tables on the Germans.

The French would bring out their chairs and sit in rows behind the wire fence, making comically appropriate remarks about the villagers and finding a nickname for each young girl. Any slight oddness in figure or dress would be noted with devastating accuracy, and it was just as well that these sallies were not understood on the far side of the wire. One of the three Frenchmen in our dormitory was an Abbé called Capdevielle, who had volunteered for the Air Service as an Observer and whose hobby was watercolour sketching. He suggested giving me lessons, but I was not a good pupil, being more concerned with airing my own views on life than in transferring the distant view from the window on to the sketching-block, and the lessons developed into discussions on a variety of topics, including that of escape.

In the early days of the camp's existence it had apparently been possible to buy from the Canteen a map of the Western Front which included the Black Forest. Railways were shown, and Vöhrenbach had been located. Only a few of these maps were actually sold, and then immediately called-in, though not before the resourceful Capdevielle had made a hasty sketch of the area between the camp and the Swiss frontier. He had, moreover, obtained from one of the French orderlies a workman's jacket with a broad yellow stripe sewn down the back, and he was in hopes of acquiring further clothes from the same source. He reckoned that, with the aid of my food parcels, the two of us should have little difficulty in covering the relatively short distance to the frontier, once we were clear of the camp itself. Here, of course, was the classic escape problem, and it remained as baffling to us as it did to the several others who were also trying to solve it.

along with a handful of other RFC men whose one idea in life was to organise an escape. This made them unpopular with some of the more senior British officers, the Regulars who had been captured during the Retreat from Mons and Le Cateau, whose training had taught them to regard capture by the enemy as one of the legitimate hazards of war. They regarded an undue interest in escape as a selfish activity which could only damage the general well-being. Such were the two schools of thought in several camps. Since I could still only walk with the aid of a stick, the possibility of escape had never crossed my mind.

The camp consisted of three separate buildings, forming three sides of a 400 yards square, surrounded by two rows of barbed wire. Two of the buildings were new and contained about 200 men each, with an average of eight in a room. The colonels had rooms to themselves, all of which were well ventilated, while the other officers shared in twos. The third building, however, in which Herbert was held, was very old and formed part of the citadel of Mainz. The tunnel-vaulted rooms were dark and dirty, with an average of 12 or 14 men to each, with beds sometimes placed one above the other.

Being the only person in that room wearing RFC wings, and having developed a habit of sitting perched on the edge of an upper bunk, I became known from then on as 'Sparrow'. There was little to complain about except that silence had now become an almost inaccessible luxury. Even the remote attic library was liable to be occupied by a Scotsman who filled the air with the deafening skirl of his pipes, and I could see myself following the example of those who committed petty misdemeanours in order to be sentenced to three days solitary confinement.

In Herbert's building there were no facilities for washing except basins in the room, while the latrines were 'disgraceful and insanitary'. They were allowed a warm shower once a week and a cold one every morning.

The food was bad; we got the following. Early morning: coffee, which was bad – not like coffee. At midday, we went to a separate dining room and had for the most part sausages, quite uneatable, and fair soup, it might have had meat in it. About six inches of black bread for the day. The next meal was supper, at 7pm in the same building, consisting of much the same as lunch, with beer and wine extra. There was a canteen, open three days a week only from 8am to 12pm and again from 3pm to 4.30pm. Jam was the only food obtainable, prices rather expensive; smoking materials and certain articles of clothing could be got. Cooking was allowed in our living rooms and so we formed a kind of mess and lived almost entirely on the contents of our parcels, which we cooked on small spirit stoves obtained from the canteen. Bread arrived regularly for us in good condition from the Red Cross at Berne. Any tinned food was kept in a cellar, and could only be opened in the presence of a German sergeant.

For exercise, we could walk about the square and we started some hockey and tennis – the net was not allowed to be string, but wire. A week or two before I left, they started walks in the town and the country round. We were in parties numbering up to 30 by nationalities, under the guard of an officer and a dozen men armed; we had to walk by threes, like a schoolgirl's crocodile. Walks lasted generally about 1½ hours and took place, for us, about once a fortnight. What little there was of the population took no notice of us at all. The streets of Mainz seemed absolutely deserted and what inhabitants we saw were invariably either old men or women; no tradesmen's carts, no horses, or motors.

At 9.30am we paraded in front of each building and were counted by a sergeant. When the numbers were checked, an officer passed down the line and we had to salute. At 4.30pm, the same again. At 8pm we were again counted in our rooms and a guard sometimes came round about midnight. Punishments consisted of solitary confinement in a cell; this was not very terrible as you could have books and food and a good bed.

Perhaps due to the large number of French prisoners, who began to arrive on a regular basis after the opening of the Battle of Verdun on 21 February, Herbert and three other British officers transferred to a new camp on the evening of Saturday 4 March. Escorted to a second-class train carriage, they travelled south through the night to Vöhrenbach, a prisoner of war camp for officers located 3,000 feet up in the Black Forest region.

It was a pleasantly snow-covered village whose inhabitants seemed a cheerful lot compared with the townsfolk at Mainz and Cologne. A hundred or so French officers were already installed in the handsome new school building, with only four British and five or six Russians. The tall thin Commandant was a surprisingly benign figure for a Prussian Colonel, and our central-heated surroundings could hardly have been more attractive. He impressed upon us that it was the best camp in Germany, and it certainly was very good. The food was better cooked and served than at Mainz; the bread was better though made of sawdust and potatoes. Jam, sardines, sweets and fruit, besides articles of clothing, on sale at the canteen.

The discipline was the same as at Mainz only the roll calls were at 10.30am and 9.30pm. You had to be present at lunch and dinner, where you were counted. There was a cell but it was not required; all were contented and well-behaved. My pay was 60 marks a month, from which 54 marks were deducted for meals, whether eaten or not. The grounds in all could not have been more than 100 square yards, which was decidedly insufficient for exercise; for recreation indoors we had a piano and two billiard tables. Smoking was allowed anywhere. Hot shower baths could be had three times a week and cold every day.

The two senior British officers, Major Godman and Captain Binney, were both in very poor health and hoped to be invalided to Switzerland, but the remaining five of us were prepared to take life light-heartedly, Newbould giving mock salutes and cheeky greetings to the stout Canteen Feldwebel, and all of us 'covering off' during Appels in such a way as to falsify the numbers.

The approach of spring encouraged the local population to take its Sunday afternoon stroll along the road that went past the prison camp. The inmates, who one might have expected to be made to feel like animals in a zoo, rather took the opportunity to turn the tables on the Germans.

The French would bring out their chairs and sit in rows behind the wire fence, making comically appropriate remarks about the villagers and finding a nickname for each young girl. Any slight oddness in figure or dress would be noted with devastating accuracy, and it was just as well that these sallies were not understood on the far side of the wire. One of the three Frenchmen in our dormitory was an Abbé called Capdevielle, who had volunteered for the Air Service as an Observer and whose hobby was watercolour sketching. He suggested giving me lessons, but I was not a good pupil, being more concerned with airing my own views on life than in transferring the distant view from the window on to the sketching-block, and the lessons developed into discussions on a variety of topics, including that of escape.

In the early days of the camp's existence it had apparently been possible to buy from the Canteen a map of the Western Front which included the Black Forest. Railways were shown, and Vöhrenbach had been located. Only a few of these maps were actually sold, and then immediately called-in, though not before the resourceful Capdevielle had made a hasty sketch of the area between the camp and the Swiss frontier. He had, moreover, obtained from one of the French orderlies a workman's jacket with a broad yellow stripe sewn down the back, and he was in hopes of acquiring further clothes from the same source. He reckoned that, with the aid of my food parcels, the two of us should have little difficulty in covering the relatively short distance to the frontier, once we were clear of the camp itself. Here, of course, was the classic escape problem, and it remained as baffling to us as it did to the several others who were also trying to solve it.

However, any notions of escape for Herbert were to be interrupted. News had reached the German authorities that certain officer prisoners in the hands of the French were not being treated in accordance with the Geneva Convention, and immediate reprisals were deemed appropriate. Since the camp at Vöhrenbach consisted almost entirely of French officers, it was thought to be the most suitable for reprisals, once the British and the Russians had been moved elsewhere. Suddenly, for Herbert, escape became a very real possibility.

The Commandant was furious, for his whole kindly policy was now to be reversed. We felt genuinely sorry for him as he stampeded about, but we also realised that the journey offered us a ready-made solution to our problem, for the train could only reach Heidelberg (our destination) after first travelling south as far as Donaueschingen, the nearest town to the Swiss frontier. All that we now had to do was to get out of that train before it started travelling north. There was no time to work out our plans in detail, but Capdevielle who, poor man, would be remaining at Vöhrenbach, made me a present of his workman's jacket (from which the yellow stripe had been removed), and I now joined forces with Champion, who had also secured a jacket, while Newbould teamed up with McKeagh. Thinking it would be easier to escape from the train by night, we made an unsuccessful attempt to delay our actual departure, but we were all wearing pseudo-civilian clothes under our service coats when taken to say goodbye to the Commandant. He seemed genuinely upset about our transfer and made a little speech to that effect in his Prussian French, ending with a 'Bon voyage!' which made me feel uncomfortably double-faced.

Around 8.30am on Monday 17 April, the prisoners began their journey.

On the way down to the station the ends of Newbould's contraband trousers began to emerge from under his flying-coat, but he somehow managed to hitch them out of sight, to everyone else's great relief. The next thing was to take stock of our railway carriage. It was small and of rustic design, having only a door at each end and three compartments within, the middle one having no means of access except from either end. A couple of burly Landwehr men stationed themselves at each of the outer doors, a bell was rung, and off we went, our arrival having probably delayed the departure of the local train. Newbould and McKeagh were in the unguarded middle compartment, while Champion and I sat in an end one with the Landwehr men and three or four Russians who spoke a little German. They had agreed that, if we saw a chance of getting through a window in the middle compartment, they would do their best to distract the guards' attention by keeping them in conversation during the critical time that this was taking place.

It would obviously have been foolish to jump out while the train was speeding along, and we hoped that it would soon have to contend with a gradient. When it stopped at a small station with only a single platform, I felt that the moment had arrived. Champion nodded, and the Russians understood. As we made our way as casually as possible into the middle compartment, they began to hobnob with the Landwehr men. To our great annoyance we found that the vital window could not be lowered more than half-way. Never mind: it was now or never. True to form, Newbould, the first to go, became wedged head downward and had to be given a heave which sent him crashing on to the track below. It was an anxious moment, but sounds of ponderous German laughter came filtering through from the end compartment, so out went McKeagh followed by Champion and myself, each of us landing with a most resounding thud.

We had agreed to travel in twos, so Newbould and McKeagh had already started off in one direction when Champion and I, as previously arranged, walked unhurriedly along the length of the train, he occasionally chatting to me in Afrikaans and I making vaguely Germanic noises in reply. I had no difficulty in feigning a limp, and Champion managed to make himself appear convincingly bow-legged, for we reckoned that anyone of military age would have been in uniform unless he were in some way physically unfit. We eventually reached the locomotive without being noticed even by the driver or his fireman, and then turned to the right along a road leading uphill into open country, the train meanwhile remaining unpleasantly motionless. There was no cover except a distant wood, and we felt that the guards, having now discovered our absence, might at this very moment be taking careful aim with their rifles, yet to hurry would have been fatal. After what seemed like an endless wait, we heard the train give a whistle and then puff slowly away. We resisted the temptation to look back, but could hardly believe that we had not been missed – yet it was true. We were now on our own, though with few provisions, no compass of any kind, and only a sketchy and far from accurate map. On the other hand, we could not be much more than 20 miles from the Swiss frontier.

Herbert and Champion soon entered woodland and lost sight of the other two escapees. Lacking a compass, they had to rely on the position of the sun for direction but aimed roughly south for the Swiss border, guided by their primitive map.

We went along in a forest, where we had to drink water out of the puddles and the cart ruts. We kept on, marking a high hill in the distance, which, according to the sun, was in the direction we wanted to go, and thought we should be able to remember what it looked like, and steer by it; but directly we turned round a corner, or went up another hill, it looked quite different, and did not help us in the least. It then began to rain. We came to a stream, which must have been the Danube, and which was just too wide to jump. We walked along parallel with it for about two hundred yards, till we came to a little bridge close to a village. We crossed over there, and on the other side were a man and a boy quite close, loading up a hay-cart. I managed to put on a limp, and Champion appeared to be bandy-legged. We just said: 'Ja, Ja wohl', as we passed them. We had to retrace our steps along the other bank, and climbed a hill on the side of which we had lunch. After that we walked on until we came to a railway line. Our greatest stroke of good fortune was the discovery that there was no need for us to negotiate the complicated double loop of railway line which lay ahead, since we had already done so, by passing over the top of a long tunnel not shown on our map.

As might have been expected, we made quite a number of mistakes, and it was not easy to maintain any sense of direction, for the sun was not visible and a drizzling rain set in, changing to sleet on higher ground. At the foot of a valley there was a signpost which pointed to 'Blumberg' and we decided that we must not go anywhere near the village. We did not seem able to avoid it, however, and soon came to a village which we thought was Blumberg but which was really Achdorf. We passed round a hill at the back of the village; we were seen by a group of people in a courtyard, who looked at us, we thought, rather suspiciously. And it must have seemed rather curious that two people without overcoats should be walking round that hill, in the pouring rain, fairly near the frontier.

The countryside was too exposed to cross by daylight. When it was dark, we went very cautiously. [Suddenly] a light was flashed on us and we thought it was all up. We fell down flat at once, and just waited for someone to shout out. The light remained quite still, however, for some time and after watching it, we decided that no one could hold it as still as that, and that it was probably some trick of the man who was coming up behind us. We looked round and saw two dark masses, which appeared exactly like two men crawling up. After looking at them for some time, however, we found that they were merely two bushes, and after further investigation we found that the light had been swung on the railway line, as there were probably repairs going on. We climbed up this hill, thinking that we were practically on the frontier, and when among the trees on the top, we jumped every time we heard a branch crack.

Having no compass, it was exceptionally difficult for the two men to establish their direction of travel, but they guided themselves by the position of a river and the direction of the wind as they trudged onwards and upwards, higher into the mountains.

We were quite high up then and the clouds were practically on the ground, so that we could only see a very short distance ahead. We fell flat down on seeing a shadow in front of us and, after waiting some time, it turned out to be a plough. We went down a valley slightly to our left, and then did not know whether to go on or not. We had noticed that the wind was from west to east and held up our handkerchiefs to see if we were still going right. It blew in exactly the opposite direction to what we thought, and we were afraid we had gone in a circle. We tried to see which side of the trees were wet, but they were damp and clammy all round.

Then we suddenly spied a little hut. We heard a noise which sounded like footsteps going past, and after having lain down on the wet leaves for about ten minutes, we decided that it was probably only the dripping of the rain and thought it was best to get shelter in the hut. I was almost sure we were in Switzerland, but Champion said we ought to be very careful and that he would not be convinced until we had walked for at least two hours in the right direction and that we were probably still in Germany. At any rate, we knocked on the door of the hut, intending to run if there had been any sound inside, and since there was none, we went inside and found it was merely a log hut with a few shelves in it, and had evidently never been inhabited. We sat down and waited. It was then about two in the morning. We took off our shoes and stockings and wrung them out. We were absolutely soaked and so cold we could hardly stand. I was in a state of complete collapse and did not much mind whether the Germans came or not; but Champion who was not so done up, got up and started a fire. After three unsuccessful attempts we got it going, and kept it alight by burning the brackets which were on the side of the hut. There was a good space between each log, and the light of that fire could have been seen for miles. The wind also came through these cracks which did not make it any warmer. We took our clothes off, toasted some bread, dried the cheese and finished off our provisions.

Time passed very quickly for Herbert and Champion in their comfortable nest, and before long they suddenly realised that dawn had broken and that it was light outside. They therefore resumed their journey rapidly, regulating their course by the sunrise.

We thought that by now we must be in Switzerland, and started to whistle and walk arm-in-arm. We came on a road which we followed, still going more or less due east. Turning a corner, we found ourselves practically in a village and, as someone looked out of a window, it was too late to turn back so we decided to keep straight on. The names, of course, were all German and there was nothing to show whether we were in Germany or Switzerland. Just as we were leaving the village, a man in uniform leant out of a window and shouted out in bad French, 'Halt, come back here', and there was nothing for us to do but to turn back. He took us into his little house which was the post office and we noticed a white cross on a red background on his cap; but we were not at all sure what he would do to us. When he asked us questions, we told him we were two civilians, an Englishman and a Frenchman, aged fifteen and sixteen, who had come from Heidelberg; but he asked us such awkward questions and we had to tell such copious lies that we eventually asked him what would happen if we said we were two British officers. 'Why, nothing at all', he said, 'I should take you into Schaffhausen and you would be escorted back to the frontier by Swiss officers'. We were still not very sure of him and asked him which frontier he meant and were very relieved when he replied, 'the French frontier'.

He then asked us to have some breakfast, and gave us some very excellent coffee and some white bread which tasted better than anything I have ever known. His wife was there fussing about, and they were both as nice as they could be. He took us along afterwards to Schaffhausen, avoiding the road, because it crosses the frontier again and he said the Germans would have a right to snatch us from him if we kept to it. If we left the road, they would have no right over us at all, though he said it was quite likely they would shoot us if they saw us. After we had walked some distance, we very luckily came upon a little car which was going into Schaffhausen, and had a lift, as we were very tired by then and I had been stumbling along all the way.

At Schaffhausen, one of the most northerly major towns in Switzerland, the two British officers were handed over to the Swiss officials responsible for policing the frontier. Despite the escapees' desire for a much longed-for bath and meal, they were immediately handed over to a local tobacconist named Blank, who could speak French.

It was very funny to hear the people talking German and realise that one was safe in spite of it. The Swiss government must have arranged for Blank to look after us, as he told us he could not let us out of his sight and insisted that we should come up and have a wash at his place, and afterwards have lunch with him. This was very annoying, as his washing arrangements only consisted of a wooden tub in a room at the top of the house, which also contained all the family washing hung up, which flapped in your face. He insisted on shampooing us himself, and raked up some clothes from somewhere. I had a black shiny suit, about two feet too big round the waist; and he fussed about it so much that I very nearly got angry with him. We finally got fixed up after a fashion and he took us off to have lunch with him and two friends; one being a man who sold oil paints and the other an undertaker. After lunch, which was quite a good one, I collapsed altogether, and went and laid down.

Eventually leaving Schaffhausen for Zurich, the two men arrived early on in the evening and were taken to an office to be interrogated by a Swiss colonel.

He wanted to hear all about us, asked the most pointless questions, was rather deaf, and took the whole story down on a typewriter which he manipulated with one finger. This took something over an hour and a half. He was very pleased with a little joke of his own. When asking us about the food in Germany he put down: 'The food, as always in Germany, was coarse'. From here, we were taken to the British Consulate, where they were very interested in us, as we were the first prisoners who had ever got through that way. At Berne, following an early start, the British Military Attaché and several other officials from the Legation were anxious to hear the story, and there was an English journalist in the train who was also full of questions. A Swiss officer in the train congratulated us very warmly and told us he was always glad to hear of people getting away from Germany. He said that when he was guarding the frontier with his patrol, he had had a most amusing experience in shooting two Germans who came across. He added that he was very pleased to be able to fire at them.

They had been told to report to the Provost-Marshal immediately on arrival in Paris, who then directed the two officers to Montreuil where they were to be officially debriefed.

We were taken to the Intelligence Corps headquarters and given breakfast at one end of an extremely long table, while our hosts in their green-tabbed uniforms sat at the opposite end without sparing so much as a glance in our direction. Puzzled by this inhospitable reception, it eventually dawned on us, during the searching interrogations which followed, that we were regarded as very suspicious characters. Only one British officer had ever escaped from Germany: a certain Major or Colonel Vandeleur, who had somehow managed to reach Denmark. The war had now been in progress for nearly two whole years, and no one else had so far succeeded in escaping, yet here were these two young civilians, neither of whom spoke German, claiming that they had jumped from a guarded

Herbert Ward (left) and Hilary Champion, in a photograph taken by the British Vice Consul at Zurich, immediately following their successful escape from Germany. Herbert is seen wearing clothes lent to him by the Consul.

train in broad daylight while it was standing at a station, and had then walked into Switzerland without having once been challenged. The thing didn't make sense: either they were imposters trying to perpetrate a hoax or they were German agents who had concocted a clumsy story. Some such ideas must presumably have been in the minds of the professional sceptics into whose hands we had fallen.

It would be Brigadier General Hugh Trenchard himself, the Officer Commanding the RFC in France, who came to their rescue and collected the men in his car, taking them to the unit's newly established headquarters at St Andre-aux-Bois.

In his way of thinking, at any rate, it was quite reasonable to expect a couple of his young flying men to give their captors the slip: it was entirely in keeping with the spirit of the RFC. 'They must have champagne!' he boomed, as we followed him into the Chateau – but alas none could be found, and it was not even possible for us to stay to lunch, as the cross-Channel boat was due to sail an hour earlier than usual. There was nevertheless time for us to be shown the photocopy of the note which I had scribbled on the Interpreter's pad soon after my capture, and which was now pasted into an album. It had been photographed by the German Air Force who had then dropped copies over our lines. Several of the Staff Officers to whom we had to report at the War Office on our return to London seemed vaguely suspicious about the escape. We received, in fact, the traditional treatment accorded to pioneers: we were given ten days' leave – hardly sufficient time to have a new uniform made – and no further recognition of any kind, either then or later.

Herbert Ward (1897–1987)

Following his demobilisation in 1919, Herbert was ordained into the Anglican clergy and became The Reverend Herbert Ward. The account of his time in captivity during the First World War was written soon after the events described, but many years later, in the 1970s, he used these contemporary records to expand upon his experiences and sought the advice of a publisher, who unfortunately believed that his written memoir had 'insufficient flamboyance'. Herbert was therefore delighted when, in 1977, the Imperial War Museum confirmed an interest in preserving his memoir and making it more widely available. Based for many years at the College of St Barnabas in Surrey, he moved to Brighton in later life where he died in 1987, aged 89.

5 | Fred

CONSCIENTIOUS OBJECTION
MARCH 1916 – 1918

There was the usual medical examination and particulars were taken. Then away to a cell to become a number

By the end of 1915, the outlook for Britain was bleak. Hopes of a swift success on the Western Front had been dashed, while the campaign at Gallipoli had been an outright failure. The country was to face a prolonged war which would necessitate further sacrifices, not only in terms of men but with regard to individual freedom. Everybody would experience greater government involvement in their day-to-day lives. Conscription was seen as a necessary step to boost the country's fighting force and hasten a decisive victory, but neither the government nor the military authorities had properly considered how they would deal with those who objected to military service for reasons of conscience. Despite the country's widespread patriotism and the popular jingoistic desire to beat the German threat, a growing number of individuals began to question the wisdom of fighting.

The Military Service Act which came into force on 2 March 1916 introduced conscription to the United Kingdom for men aged between 18 and 41. Those who appealed against military service would face locally established tribunals who were to decide between 'conscience or cowardice'. It was down to the individual objector to demonstrate proof of their beliefs before the tribunal which, considering the intangible nature of a person's conscience, was a far from straightforward task.

One such objector to conscription was Frederick James Murfin, a 27 year-old Quaker living in Tottenham, north London. Along with other members of the Religious Society of Friends, Fred believed strongly in the principles of peace and non-violence, while the Quaker avoidance of rigid creeds and organisational structures meant that any adherence to military discipline would also be against his principles. Fred received his first notice on Wednesday 8 March 1916, ordering him to report to the local Town Hall.

My case was eventually heard on March 23rd. It was a terrible ordeal to anyone sensitive; I found it very trying. How does one feel when trying in public to convince people (who are out to trip up and misconstrue anything one says) that because of one's religious convictions – no matter what the consequences – no war service is possible? I was asked by a member of the Tribunal what my occupation was and I replied that I was a printer. He further asked if I was printing for export (which might mean an exemption or postponement). I replied that I was objecting on religious grounds. I was given a Non-combatant Certificate, but I said that I would not take it and would appeal. Next came the Appeal Tribunal held at the Guildhall, Westminster. The Military Representative asked if I would kill wild beasts. I replied, 'The Germans are not wild beasts, sir!' The non-combatant orders were confirmed. Anyone who refused to join up was termed a Deserter and I awaited arrest.

Within four months the Military Service Act had created only 43,000 new recruits – while 93,000 men had failed to attend the recruiting office when called upon, and a massive 748,587 had requested exemption from military service and were to face tribunals. Tribunals were usually very harsh towards the men whom society at that time commonly regarded as shirkers. Hearsay and personal opinion were admissible as evidence against them, while members of tribunals were overwhelmingly middle-class and working in the interests of local government; as such, they were wholeheartedly behind the national cause of finding able-bodied men to fight.

From March 1916 – when Fred Murfin faced his tribunal – until the end of the war, only 16,100 men were recognised as conscientious objectors and allocated alternative service 'of national importance'. Such work was primarily unarmed service in the Non-Combatant Corps or civilian labour such as farm or factory work, and was accepted in the majority of cases. Failure to comply with such duties would mean arrest and imprisonment. No more than 200 men, a very small percentage, would receive absolute exemption from military service.

Sunday, May 21st 1916, was a landmark in my life. After attending Tottenham Friends' Meeting I went back to my lodging, and after dinner my landlord asked me to go into the garden with him for a talk. 'Oh!' I said, 'has the policeman been?' The officer had been told where I was and that if he would say when he would call again, I would be in. He came again on the Monday evening and after a chat said, 'Well – you know what I have come for?' 'Yes', I said. 'Will you meet me at the police station tomorrow, or would you like a few days to arrange matters?' I said that if it was alright for him I would have a few days, and we agreed that I should report at Tottenham Police Station on Thursday morning, May 25th.

I went to work as usual on Tuesday and Wednesday. I had to decide whether I should continue my work or go to Louth, Lincolnshire, to say goodbye to my parents. This experience seemed unreal to me and I carried on as usual, which seemed the right thing to do at the time. On the Sunday evening after the policeman had called, I went along as usual to the Friends evening meeting and told my friends there and said goodbye to them. Some promised to be along at the police court and to write letters, which they did. I wrote to tell my parents what was happening, and on Thursday morning I reported to the Tottenham police. I was put in a cell but the door was not locked. Soon after six on the same evening, more Conscientious Objectors were brought in from

Edmonton. One I already knew, Stuart Beavis. While we were in the cells a Belgian was brought in who was in trouble with the police; also, a deserter – an indignant Irishman who had a lot to say for himself.

Particulars were taken at the Police Station and then we were taken to the Magistrate's Court. Several of my friends were there. At this court we were charged individually as 'Deserters from the Army'. I declared my faith, was found guilty and fined 40/-d or fourteen days. No one paid any fine and the fourteen days meant nothing. We were then taken under escort to Mill Hill Recruiting Station.

Particulars were again taken – by a junior officer. We were then sent (or taken) for medical examination and told to strip. We were told that if we didn't, our clothes would be torn off! We found we would be putting our clothes on again, so we did strip. But I was as unhelpful as I knew how to be – kept my feet on the ground when weighed; told the Eye Doctor I couldn't help him and the Heart Doctor the same thing, telling each that I was a Conscientious Objector and wouldn't be a soldier.

Soon after this we were taken to the stores for uniform. Kit bags were put around our necks. I refused to give the size of anything and the men had to guess. All the things were piled into the bag – such a one as I associated with sailors. As I wouldn't carry the thing, the bag was hung around my neck; then one man on either side and one behind ran me to another department, pressing on the bag and nearly strangling me. Had I been less nervous I would have refused to use my legs. When I arrived, gasping for breath, the officer there was very concerned. My throat (Adam's apple) still hurts if I press it slightly, nearly forty-five years after. Stuart Beavis was treated in the same way.

Opposition to the war was most definitely a minority view. From early on in the war, a campaign of shaming men to enlist by presenting them with a white feather if they were not in uniform had helped to create a situation in which every man needed to be seen to be 'doing his bit', and any nonconformity could lead to mockery, insult or, in the worst cases, violence.

Next came the putting on of the uniform. We all refused, I think, and we each had a soldier to undress and dress us. My attendant suggested that as my feet smelled so badly I'd better see to my own socks! I did and we both enjoyed the joke. He was a nice fellow – we found, as a rule, that if the officer was decent, the men were. We were taken back to the Guardroom and saw one another in uniform for the first time. One man came in later very flustered. He had resisted having the uniform put on and his words were: 'They have got the uniform on but they haven't got the man!' We tried to help him to accept the situation and pointed out that we were still prisoners.

For tea we had bread and butter and a bucket of tea which we drank out of a basin. I remember that whilst we were at Mill Hill, one young man had a letter from his father who wrote that his mother had become ill through thinking of her son as a coward because he wouldn't go to be a soldier. I didn't know his name or what happened to him.

Justifications for refusing to fight were many and varied. The most common argument was that war and the act of killing were inconsistent with the basis of most religious teaching. Many conscientious objectors followed this conviction despite their respective churches often supporting the government's position. Others made a political argument against the war. This was the age when socialism was growing in importance, and war was deemed to have no place in a truly socialist society. Some regarded the conflict as a result of political manoeuvrings rather than having a clear moral purpose. Within this range of beliefs, individual attitudes varied dramatically. Some objected to any form of fighting, while others opposed only the current conflict; some, such as Fred, would refuse any cooperation with the authorities, while others would eventually embrace active participation as stretcher bearers or munitions workers.

The next morning we had breakfast and, not more than an hour later, dinner was brought in and we were told to be quick as we

*were to march to the station. We lined up and were put behind a
lot of non-combatant men; we were under escort. Occasionally an
officer would tell us to keep in step, but we took no notice – though
curiously enough we soon seemed to be unconsciously in step. We
kept, deliberately, getting out of it!*

*We reached Mill Hill station long before the train was due. We
were going to Seaford and had to change at Lewes. Our escorts
asked if we would sign for our day's pay, then they could buy food
for us. Unless we did sign, they said, neither we nor they could have
food. But we wouldn't sign anything.*

Despite his protests, Fred was being treated as a military conscript who
would see service in the Non-Combatant Corps – whether he liked it or not.

*We reached Seaford Camp late in the afternoon. An officer chatted with
us and said they had no trouble with Conscientious Objectors. The
non-combatant men were very happy there, he said, and did odd jobs
gardening and attending to paths. If we fell in with the rest, 'All our crimes
would be wiped out'. We would start with a clean sheet. We repeated: 'We
shall refuse to obey all military orders on conscientious grounds.' We were
taken off to the guard-room and found it full of CO's, and were told that
there were more CO's in another guard-room. One of the non-combatant
men told us he had meant to stand out, but he was alone and gave in. He
wished he could join us. But if he had refused to obey orders he would
not have kept with us. When we had settled in the guard-room we talked
among ourselves and felt that we had stood our ground.*

*When we were at this camp we saw men having bayonet-practice
and throwing mock bombs. I heard of one man who couldn't do this
bayonet-practice – he was vomiting so badly. They had to give him some
other military duty. Everybody should see this disgusting practice.*

Now officially part of the military organisation, Fred and his fellow
conscientious objectors were liable for court martial if found guilty

of disobeying military orders. The findings of the court martial could range from minor punishments for those serving in this country or, if found guilty in the war zone itself, the death penalty could apply.

May 28th 1916, when evidence was taken for the court martial, was a very hot day. We stood outside for hours awaiting our turn. The Lieutenant who took my particulars had only one arm. He was very abusive and told me he had lost his arm defending me. I replied, 'You lost your arm whilst you were trying to destroy someone else!' This made him mad. He kept calling me Private Murfin. I said I wasn't a Private. He said I was. I said I wasn't. We repeated this a few times, then I said, 'You may think I am but I am not a Private. I'm a prisoner'. The only particulars I gave him was my name. He filled the paper up as best he could – it was not my concern.

The following day, an officer announced that the new conscripts were to be sent to France. If Fred and his fellow conscientious objectors refused to go willingly, they would be handcuffed and placed under escort in the manner of prisoners. The Army was proceeding to send them nearer to the combat zone in order to discourage any further resistance; the consequences for disobeying orders on active service were significantly more severe.

We were lined up outside the guard-room. A kit bag was fixed on each of us and things put in it, with comments: 'A razor – they'll cut their throats before they're through!' A paybook: 'They'll want their pay alright!', and so on. I used my paybook as a diary. Some filled them with texts and others threw them away when their hands were free. Any left were taken away from us. Our hands were handcuffed behind our backs. An officer came up to me and, speaking friendly enough, said, 'You know my lad, it's a Christian duty to fight for your country in war time' – quoting the Old Testament. I replied quoting the New Testament and he laughed, shook hands with me and wished me luck.

Well, each of us had an escort and I said to mine, 'Give me a push or I won't walk'. 'All right, mate!' he answered, and we set off. We were behind the non-combatant men, who seemed very downhearted. As we started, one of the escorts kept tripping one of the younger lads. 'If you don't stop that', I called out, 'We will refuse to walk'. He stopped. We hadn't gone far when we stopped for some unknown reason. I learned afterwards that Stuart Beavis had decided not to walk (why hadn't we all thought of that?). In the struggle Stuart's glasses were broken, and they had to get a conveyance and lift him into it.

Seaford is a terminus and the train was in the station, so we got in with our escorts, who took our kit bags off so that we could sit down. The officer in charge came to ask if we would have our handcuffs off. Before the train started he came again – the same reply: 'No!' At the first stop he came and asked if we would have them off as a favour to him? I said, 'Yes, if they are put on again before we leave the train'. I suppose he felt uncomfortable about us.

We eventually arrived at Southampton Quay, the handcuffs were put on and we stood together on the platform, left till last. I suggested that we ask to see the officer in command before we went on board and make our protest. We all agreed. When he arrived we said: 'We are religious conscientious objectors to all warfare, and we shall refuse to obey all military orders and shall only move under escort. We are prisoners, not soldiers.' We asked him to report our protest, and he said that he would do so. We thanked him and said that we would move so long as we had an escort.

As we went on board the 'St Tudno' we were hooted, and shouts of 'Put them amongst the Australians or Canadians!' were heard. I believe the hooters were non-combatant men who had accepted that service. Well, we were put among these colonials, and having got our kit off had started to talk to them when we were moved down to the ship's hold. There we found sixteen COs from Richmond, Yorkshire, who had arrived before us.

The 'Richmond Sixteen' and Fred's group of nine from Seaford were part of a larger body of some 50 men who had been ordered to be sent to France. This decision is likely to have been made in order to threaten the men and discourage further military disobedience, while setting a useful example to those of a similar mind still in England who might be considering their own objection to conscription. Either way, the fate of Fred and his comrades would prove instrumental in deciding future policy.

We talked until we fell asleep, in all sorts of positions, and awoke to find that we had arrived at Le Havre. Before leaving the ship, we got together in our separate groups to decide on our next move, and I suggested that we refuse to leave the ship till we had, again, made our protest and demanded an escort. We walked to a camp at Le Havre and stayed there till towards evening. At this camp I saw a man who had been given absolute exemption at the first Tribunal (we were members of the same NCF branch). The military representative had appealed; the second Tribunal had taken the exemption away and the man had accepted non-combatant service.

Evening came and we walked to Le Havre goods station and entrained, travelling through the night to Rouen. There we sat about the goods yard and then entrained again, travelling at night to Bologne. This train was a tremendous length, and often we went for some distance at walking pace. Some of us got out and picked wild flowers, then ran and caught the train up. We could see a nice house in the distance with roses blooming, and I thought of my own roses at home. Some of the soldiers went into an orchard and pulled small uneatable apples – they must have been uneatable, for it was May / June. We travelled in what I know as a 'box wagon', and we had the doors open. We sat on the floor (the only place) and on one occasion I helped a soldier, one of our escorts, to get into the wagon. He passed his gun up to me and without thinking (it all seemed so unreal) I took the gun and then helped him up. But I wiped my hands afterwards!

When we arrived at Bologne we were taken to a large hut. From time to time an officer would come up and ask names. 'If you will sign here all your crimes will be wiped out.' It was quite a ritual, but we repeated that we would not sign anything. Whilst we were in this camp our party of seven or eight were allowed out on parole in the camp itself, though the other men from Richmond were allowed on parole in the town. Three of our party were walking about in the camp the day after we arrived when some soldiers asked who we were and where from. We said we were Conscientious Objectors and prisoners. They said a lot of COs had been shot the week before at this camp. We knew there had been about sixteen COs ahead of us. Anyhow it made no difference to our determination to refuse to obey military orders.

A few weeks before, a batch of 17 conscientious objectors originally held at Landguard Fort in Suffolk were the first to be sent forcibly to France, embarking on 7 May. Threatened with certain death if found to be disobeying military orders, their fate was the cause of much rumour.

We had little discussions among ourselves as to what we should do, and did what we could to encourage any who seemed to be wavering or a bit frightened. One man, whom we knew as Billy, didn't take part in any discussions, and while we were talking would dress himself up in coats turned inside out, or anything he could get hold of; a proper Bohemian. When we had been at Bologne for a few days we were told that in the morning [it was now Sunday 4 June] we would be ordered out to go to work at the docks, unloading goods. There would be a bugle call; if we didn't go we would be court-martialled and it would mean the death penalty, as we were in the war zone (we could hear gunfire occasionally). In the morning the bugle call was sounded. We could hear someone moving and were concerned as to who and how many had gone out. It was Billy. Later when we were in the guard-room and Billy brought our rations he said: 'You men have religions, I have nothing.'

When we had been in the guard-room for a few days some of us became lousy. As early as possible in the morning we would go into the

yard and start hunting – shirts off. Body lice are called 'Chats' and we
went Chatting! I was very fortunate and only caught three at the most at
any one time. Some caught many more. We asked to see the Officer in
Command and told him of our condition, and from then on we not only
had a bath but went out on exercise. The bath had its humorous side. We
sat one in each end of a bath flavoured with strong disinfectant, while
our clothes were fumigated. After the bath, a pretty picture we looked
in dressing jackets and any old thing until our clothes were ready! The
exercise, too, was very welcome. We were taken on to the hills and we
could see the cliffs of Dover. We ran and jumped, played Leap Frog and,
well, imagine a lot of healthy, energetic men having been prisoners for
some time. We made the best of it.

In the meantime we were formally committed for Court Martial
and we gave our reply that we would not obey orders on conscientious
grounds. We were given pen and paper to write out our statement,
and in due course we had our Field General Court Martial. We were
told that it would mean the supreme penalty – the death penalty.

The day arrived and we were all put in an army hut, and waited
for hours. The only exercise we could think of was Leap Frog. Very
soon we found the asbestos lining smashed up by our play, so we
used the bits as marbles for a game. If this sounds silly or frivolous,
think of a lot of healthy young men shut within four walls for a long
time, waiting for we knew not what. Looking back it seems a natural
reaction. About the Field General Court Martial I remember one
thing – something that was impressed on the minds of all of us. This
was the evidence given by a sergeant as our reply to the charge, when
he gave it to us in the charge-room. This was: 'He said he couldn't
take part in any military duties on conscientious grounds, or words
to that effect.' The phrase 'words to that effect' was on our lips on
many occasions after this.

After our Court Martial, when the rest of the men were asleep,
Stuart and I lay awake discussing what we thought might happen to
us. At the time, we thought that the first COs had been shot, and it

seemed to us probable that one or two of us might be shot and the rest given another trial. It was two or three days after this that we learned the truth behind the rumour.

On their arrival in France, the 17 men from Landguard Fort had been sentenced to death for refusing to obey military orders.

The officer told us that the death sentence had been read out, and that the men turned white (they were white already!). There was a pause, then the sentence was 'Commuted to ten years penal servitude.' I have mentioned before that we had been told they had been shot. This was the first true news we had heard, and it meant also that this was probably the sentence that we ourselves would receive.

While their death sentence had been commuted to ten years imprisonment, this decision was only made after a Non-Combatant Corps man travelling in the same train as the objectors had managed to throw a note from the carriage window to reveal their plight. Through various means the issue was raised directly with the prime minister and a reprieve by the authorities was forthcoming. Subsequent conscientious objectors facing a court martial, including Fred, would therefore benefit from this decision while sharing the same fate of incarceration.

In due course we were called out to receive our sentence. There was quite a parade of soldiers and the 'high ups' were in state. The men who had been in another camp had joined us, and as we all knew by now of the sentence that the earlier men had received, we expected, and received, the same. When the sentence was read out one man smiled (one of the youngest of us) and was reprimanded by the Big Noise. We never knew the latter's name. When we got back to the guard-room, the soldier prisoners, most of whom were already friendly with us, wanted to know the verdict. One man said he had been in prison and advised us to learn the Morse Code so that we could speak to each other if we were in adjoining cells. Two taps for a dot and one for a dash. He told us the code and soon we knew it and would practise speaking to one another in Morse Code. It was an interest and worthwhile later on – besides, it was fun.

Several days after we were sentenced we were moved to Detention Barracks. I remember that one soldier stared at Stuart, who stared back, and as a result Stuart was taken away and we didn't know why. However he soon came back and we all went off to Bologne Station, travelling in the night to Rouen and then to camp and were put in cells. There were so many of us – there were four in some cells and when we lay down we were touching each other. The cell floors were newly cemented and we had no board to lie on, just one greatcoat and, of course, we were wearing our uniform. When we got up in the morning the floor was wet. We complained, after which boards were given us and one man was taken out. Now the condition of these cells was bad. We were let out only once a day for a short time. There was no lavatory accommodation and a sort of wide bucket served the purpose. Our nerves were affected, and one of us was costive and another loose – the loose friend would say 'Sorry chaps, I'll have to do it again'.

We spent three days in the cells at Rouen, and on the fourth day we were taken to the quay and soon a ship came alongside – the 'St Tudno' – the ship we had sailed in from Southampton to Le Havre. While we waited for the men to disembark, we were aware of a crowd of people on the quay, watching. There was some commotion which I noticed but did not understand until later. A French officer called out to the crowd: 'These men are cowards. They won't fight for their King and Country. Push them in the river!'

Fortunately, Bert Brocklesby and others within Fred's group had an understanding of French and quickly realised what was about to occur. Speaking to a little boy who stood watching nearby, Bert explained that they were 'trying to follow the Lord Jesus' and, by the boy running among the people explaining who the English captives were, they avoided any further trouble.

When the ship was empty we were told to go on board and stay on deck, which pleased us. We sailed down the Seine and went below when it became dark, arriving at Southampton in the morning, July 6th. As we came off the ship and walked to the quay there was a crowd of people booing – they all seemed to be in uniform and must have been told who we were. We were taken by train to Winchester and from train to prison – just over six weeks after our arrest. We were relieved to find that we were to be in a civil prison, as this meant we would be able to do some work. The first sixteen men were already there, and this was the first time we had seen them. And so, on July 7th 1916, we arrived at Winchester Prison to carry out our sentence – the Death Penalty, commuted to ten years penal servitude.

Fred Murfin was among the 985 men who were determined to hold out for absolute exemption from military service throughout the war. Refusing to recognise the decision of the tribunals or the military orders they received as non-combatants, such individuals were known as 'Absolutists', and endured repeated terms of imprisonment under sentence of hard labour.

We arrived at Winchester Prison on July 7th 1916. Up to this time we were in military uniform; for six weeks we had worn nothing else and had only had those clothes off twice – for a bath. Winchester was our first experience of a civilian prison. And we were in England. We were all put into a reception room and, after a bath, into prison clothes. There was the usual medical examination and particulars were taken. Then away to a cell to become a number. I was C3/31, No. 31 on the third landing of C Hall. A disc was worn on the coat front with the cell number on. This was our means of identity.

It all seemed unreal at first, but one settled down and made the best of it. There were tasks of some sort in all prisons. In Maidstone there were working parties: Cookhouse, Laundry, Builders, Tin shop, Printing,

Tailoring and so on. The food was the same, with slight alterations, every week. All breakfasts:

    1 pt unsweetened porridge
    8 oz brown bread
    ¼ oz margarine (have you ever tried to spread ¼ oz of
        margarine on 8 oz of bread?)

All suppers were served about 5 o'clock and that was the last time the door was unlocked until morning, and this meal consisted of:

    1 pt ship's cocoa, slightly sweetened
    8 oz bread
    ¾ oz margarine

Dinners:

    Sunday – Corned beef
    Monday – Beans and fat bacon
    Tuesday – Braised beef
    Wednesday – Beef stew
    Thursday – Braised mutton
    Friday – Mutton stew
    Saturday – Suet pudding (no sweetening).

Potatoes each meal, cooked in their jackets – usually dirty. Occasionally we had cabbage; one year, in the summer, there was a generous supply of caterpillars. Once or twice a year coarse Cos Lettuce, just as it was pulled up, and occasionally spring onions, also dirty, were thrown into the cell with soil on. When there was a bread shortage we had very salty fish in brine for dinner, the result being that so many prisoners were ill that that didn't last long. Several of us went on a Vegetarian Diet. At first we had some rice pudding with some milk and a little sweetening, but very soon it was just rice, boiled – no flavouring.

Prisoners are weighed on arrival and a record is kept and we were weighed periodically. If there was a loss of weight, extra food was given. One of our number lost weight and he was given more food. He didn't want it. I always had sufficient, except when I was on punishment.

Privileges which might otherwise be taken for granted – such as visits from family and friends, and the sending and receipt of post – were dependent on a marking system, which was designed to encourage good behaviour among the prison inmates.

Diligent prisoners received 8 marks a day. For breaking of rules a prisoner might have so many days Solitary Confinement on bread and water (8 oz only a day), no mattress and a loss of 50 or more marks. It was an offence to speak to another prisoner and if he were reported, the offence was 'for forcing conversation on another' or, not for speaking out of the window, but for 'shouting', etc. Sounds more criminal!

I had one visit. It was a tremendous strain on my parents and myself. I had no more. There was a wire partition in front of both parties and a space between, where a warder listened to all that was said. When a prisoner had been 'inside' several years, he was able to write and receive a letter every fortnight if he had no visits. After three years in prison, a much-valued privilege was that of Talking Exercise on Sunday afternoons on the exercise grounds. Through my cell window I could watch the men talking and, towards the end of the time, arranging who to talk to next week.

There is a Church of England Chaplain at each prison. The Winchester chaplain was a bully. I only remember him visiting me twice in my cell. He once, in his sermon, told of a Conscientious Objector who was faced with several armed Germans at the front. This CO snatched a bayonet and killed everyone. We all burst out laughing – which woke up the warder. In Winchester the warders sat perched up above on a pedestal chair and usually slept during the sermon. We enjoyed the hymn-singing, and it was a welcome change to be together and away from the cell.

As an Absolutist, Fred refused to indulge in any work which related directly to the cause of the war, even to the extent of avoiding material of military origin or that was intended for use by one or other of the services.

We were pleased to have work to do and were given bags to make. When we asked what they were, we were told they were wartime mail bags. After a few days, one man got some material with 'For Naval Use' stamped on it. He stopped work and tapped in Morse code to Bert Brocklesby and told him what he had found. Then he rang for the warder and said he had stopped work and why. Bert Brocklesby went on exercise and told all he could and said 'I've stopped work'. I replied, 'So have I'. Reporting to the Governor, I said I wouldn't do military work and had been told these bags were for naval use. He said he didn't know it was military work and I was not allowed to speak to other prisoners.

I got two days punishment – bred and water in a punishment cell – solitary confinement. These cells were on ground level, never cleaned out and smelt awful. There was a stool to sit on and one was allowed out for toilet once a day. Each night clothing was taken outside and there was just a bed board to lie on – no mattress. I was back in my cell after two days; it was the weekend. I heard some COs talking out of the window and they were saying they hadn't seen Bert and Stuart and Fred. So I said through my window, 'I've been in Chokee [punishment] two days and I'll be in again tomorrow because I won't do military work'. In the morning I was reported again. I was first charged with 'Shouting out of the window'. Then I was charged with refusal to work. I said again, 'I will not do military work', resulting this time in three days solitary confinement on bread and water. I was put in a different cell this time and when the warder lifted the spy cap to see if I was all right I noticed the glass was missing, so I looked later and could see bales of canvas marked 'For Naval Use'. I didn't eat anything those three days.

Fred resumed work on sewing mail bags, this time with assurance from the prison officials that his work was intended purely for domestic use. Whether or not this was actually the case is, of course, questionable.

We COs had no opportunity to discuss things among ourselves. From the [cell] window I could see a stretch of countryside. I would make my bed and then place the table near the window with my stool on top and sit looking out until nearly dark. It was summer time. Each night I could hear someone at the opposite window and drew back as I did not want to be caught talking again, but one night he got up so quietly that I didn't hear him. He said he had been trying to catch me several nights and we talked a long time. He said he had been thinking he had made a mess of his life and he had prayed to the Virgin Mary to help him to make a fresh start. I'll never forget that. I couldn't see his face although he said he recognised me on the exercise ground. I never recognised him.

The occasional amusing incident, however, helped to lift their morale.

While we were at Winchester we were all collected and taken to have our fingerprints and our photos taken. We put on a jacket and high collar and tie. I think we all enjoyed this episode. It wasn't often we had a change like that.

Wednesday 27 September saw Fred and his fellow objectors moved from Winchester prison to Maidstone, which involved a circuitous journey to Kent in stages, via north London.

We stayed one night at Pentonville Prison – that's a wretched place. We were given oakum to pick. We had no exercise and the food was poor. When we got to London we were put on a chain, handcuffed to it. I was close to a man reputed to have won the VC. He thought it was scandalous that we should be treated like that. I said, 'I wish we could walk all over London so that folk could see how convicts are treated'. Of course I didn't enjoy the experience. We were standing in full view of the public in the middle of London.

On reaching Maidstone Prison we went through the usual routine and were fitted out with new suits. We now wore knee breeches and stockings. I became 'Convict Q259'. 'Q' represents the year 1916. There was one man at Maidstone [classified] 'D' which meant he had been in prison thirteen years, and he looked it. Maidstone, an old prison, was a Star Convict Prison for men and a local prison for women. There were two Halls. 'A' Hall was condemned long ago, I was told. The division between the cells was corrugated iron and the door had a space of about four inches at the bottom and occasionally a cat would visit us. He once jumped on my bed when I was asleep and I flung him off, not realising what it was – he never came to me again. A hammock was fastened to either side and anyone turning over in bed would shake his neighbour on either side. This Hall was very cold in winter. Slow combustion stoves were the only heat we had. I sat on the table with my feet on the stool out of reach of the draught and with the rug round me. I used to fold the rug first and put it on the concrete floor, take my shoes off and skip until I was aglow, then get fixed up on the table. 'B' Hall was more modern and had a hot (warm) water pipe though one end. I moved to 'B' Hall for about the last year while I was there. While we were in Maidstone there were several noisy air raids and as a safety precaution all upstairs prisoners were moved to ground level – making three in a cell.

One advantage to being imprisoned at Maidstone was access to library books.

We had a Bible and Prayer Book and 'Smiles' Self Help', till we changed the last-named for a novel or 'educational' book. Sympathisers sent in books and we could have books sent in. The rules said that such books would, on the prisoner's discharge, become prison property, but the sort of book the COs would have sent in would be considered unfit for ordinary convicts. One Sunday at Maidstone there was a merry event just above me. One man had tried to push a library book along the floor to the man next door and it had gone too far out. That would mean punishment for both I expect.

Maidstone Prison allowed Fred to meet a wider variety of convicts, who had been condemned to prison for many different offences.

There were several Germans inside, one a gifted linguist. Also there was an Arab with only a word or two of English. He was allowed to send a petition to the Home Secretary; 'pertish' he called it. The German helped in this instance. The German went to see the Governor and said if his dinner was not kept hot he would not help in any further translations. Of course after that the dinners were kept hot. There was a young Russian in the prison and Stuart Beavis got a Russian grammar and learned a bit in order to speak with him from time to time as he passed on exercise. Later it was discovered that the Russian was innocent and he was released. Another man near me was a Spaniard, in for spying. As he knew no English he was asking for it.

It would be a mistake to think of all convicts as hardened criminals, i.e. hopelessly anti-social. There were three doctors 'in' for illegal operations; a postman who 'didn't know what he was thinking of' when he pinched postal orders; a bank manager who lost – or found – several thousand pounds. There were a lot of soldiers and dirty criminals, some old and feeble men who just hobbled about on exercise in the centre of the yard. One man said he was 'in' for attempting to murder Lloyd George. He said he hadn't, but would have done if he could. But the man didn't look vicious.

We saw the horrible sight of two men wearing chains and parti-coloured dress. The chains hung from the waist to the ankle on either side and were welded to an iron ring at the waist and the ankles, clanging as the men walked. The dress is alternate khaki and black. This punishment was for striking an officer or escaping. The chain would be worn for a year or so, then taken off and the parti-coloured dress worn for so long, say for twelve months. The chains must have been horribly cold at night, especially in winter, for the clothes were taken away at night as they were for ordinary punishment.

Fred Murfin would spend almost three years in prison for having opposed military conscription. Throughout his captivity, he and his fellow prisoners received almost no news on the course of the war and so, when the conclusion of the conflict approached towards the end of 1918, the announcement came as a great surprise.

The day before Armistice Day, a warder told me it was thought the Armistice would be signed and if so we would all be assembled on the exercise ground and the Governor would give the news. This was the first time I had heard such a thing might happen. We were duly assembled and the good news was heard. The Arab I mentioned earlier threw his cap in the air and said 'We win, we win'.

Fred, along with other conscientious objectors, was not released from prison initially. He had to wait until April 1919 for the long hoped-for day to finally arrive.

When some of our group had some inkling of the imminence of our release they refused to have their hair cut, and their people had sent their clothes. We were all up together to see the doctor. I asked what it was all about and was told – we are going out. It was the first I had heard of the possibility. All but three had had clothes sent to the prison and they went out. Three of us were sent back to our cells and not allowed on exercise. I had a humorous novel but understandably I could not read it. After a while a warder opened my cell door very noisily and shouted at me, then whispered, 'There's a man on his way from London with suits for you three men – good luck lad and goodbye'. Then he shouted at me so that anyone outside could hear. After a while we were all moved to the gate and there were Ted Bigland, whom I knew, and Ted Mason. They had brought four suits to fit three men and what a job we had – then we were out!

Yes, we were out, on a Saturday evening. On to Maidstone station for the first railway ride for nearly three years. And with our rail fare paid to wherever we wanted to go, and for all of us it was HOME. When we reached London, two of us were unable to get a train to our destination till the Sunday morning. Ted Bigland took me to his home where he and his wife, Emily, gave us hospitality till next day – a service they had given to other COs – and it was very much appreciated. Before we went to bed we were asked what we would like for breakfast: PORRIDGE, PLEASE! They laughed and said that all the other COs had said the same.

Despite their common portrayal at the time as cowards, the bravery and determination shown by conscientious objectors in standing up for their beliefs led to many people, including soldiers and politicians, developing an admiration for their behaviour. Perhaps their greatest long-term achievement was an increased public acceptance of the legitimacy of questioning violence and war.

On Sunday morning a friend took me well on the way to King's Cross and I was on the last lap. The train seemed very slow – a familiar journey and great expectations at the end of it. I was bound for Louth, Lincolnshire, where my parents lived. I was out of the train before it stopped, ran to give up my ticket and then ran most of the way home. I looked in the front window and heard Mother say to Dad: 'There's the train! He may be on it!' A cherished memory; we had three years to talk about.

Fred Murfin (1888–1971)

After the war and his release from prison, Fred Murfin returned to London where he worked as a printer for the Caledonian Press until the late 1930s. Throughout this time, he and his wife Mavis continued to attend regular meetings in Tottenham of the Quaker Society of Friends. He took on the role of caretaker at a number of buildings and, following his wife's death and his own retirement in 1959, he moved from London to a cottage in Cornwall where he pursued a hobby of gardening. Remaining a confirmed Quaker for his entire life, he continued to attend the local Friends Meeting up until his death. He died at home in 1971, aged 83.

6 | Kit

THE BATTLE OF JUTLAND
MAY – JUNE 1916

*There was a huge sheet of flame, and then the
awful pall of yellow smoke, and the ship was gone.
There were no survivors*

British dominance of the sea through a strong and effective Royal
Navy had begun to be challenged in the years immediately preceding
the First World War, when from the 1890s Germany had started
to build its own fleet of battleships. The development of HMS
Dreadnought, launched in 1906, saw a new revolutionary design
characterised by a steam turbine propulsion system and a heavy
calibre of armaments. Germany soon responded with its own similar
ship designs and a 'naval race' developed, with Britain and Germany
striving to develop the most powerful fleet of 'dreadnoughts'. The
naval supremacy enjoyed by the British Empire for so many years
was to be put under serious threat.

The outbreak of war resulted in two relatively minor naval battles,
both taking place in the North Sea which Britain prudently guarded
in order to protect its merchant shipping from enemy attack. A naval
blockade of Germany had been put into operation in August 1914,
and at the end of that month naval patrols were attacked off the
north-west coast of Germany during the Battle of Heligoland Bight.
The Battle of Dogger Bank on 24 January 1915 had seen squadrons
of the British Grand Fleet and German High Seas Fleet clash for the

first time, although on that occasion only one German ship was lost. It was perhaps inevitable that a more decisive action would take place in the North Sea – although it would not be until 1916, when Admiral Reinhard Scheer took over command of the German fleet, that a more aggressive naval strategy began to be advocated.

Meanwhile, as the Senior Service, the Royal Navy remained the career of choice for many young men in Britain. Among them was Clifford 'Kit' Caslon who, at the age of 20 in January 1916, had been appointed as a Sub Lieutenant to the newly commissioned battleship HMS *Malaya*. On completion of its sea trials at the beginning of February, the ship immediately joined the 5th Battle Squadron of fast super-dreadnoughts intended to act as the vanguard of the main battle line. The first few months of 1916 were spent at Scapa Flow doing exercises, but by the end of May the 5th Battle Squadron had been sent to Rosyth and, on the evening of Tuesday 30 May, proceeded to the North Sea as part of the Battlecruiser Fleet under the command of Vice-Admiral Sir David Beatty. The squadron consisted of the flagship HMS *Barham*, HMS *Valiant*, HMS *Warspite* and Kit's *Malaya*.

In the interim, German battlecruisers under the command of Vice-Admiral Franz Hipper had already been ordered to sea, their plan being to lure the British Navy into the direct path of the German High Seas Fleet and strike a decisive and symbolic blow against British dominance, breaking the naval blockade in the process. Intelligence of the plan had previously reached Admiral Sir John Jellicoe, and the British Grand Fleet was therefore already at sea, intent to join forces with Beatty's battlecruiser squadrons and engage the enemy. Locating the German fleet was far from straightforward, however, and it was not until the afternoon of Wednesday 31 May that Beatty's battlecruisers encountered Hipper's force, just off the Danish Jutland Peninsula.

Kit Caslan was assigned to the morning watch in *Malaya* and, after lunch, had seized the opportunity of two hours' sleep in the gunroom armchair.

**Kit Caslon, in a photograph taken around the time
of his naval service in *HMS Malaya***

*I was woken by some excited conversation on the part of the
midshipmen. One of them had just come down from the bridge, and
said there was a 'buzz' that a German destroyer had been sighted by
'someone somewhere' – it didn't sound very promising. The steward
was laying the table for tea, but we never sat down to it, as just at
3.30 the bugles sound for 'Action' and we all ran to our stations.
From that moment events happened very rapidly.*

Kit's action station was the starboard gun control tower (abbreviated
to GCT), an armoured position at the side of the conning tower

and about 30 feet above the battery on the main deck, which consisted of six 6-inch guns. His duty was to control the gunfire of this battery, under the direction of a Principal Control Officer in the foretop. With each GCT only big enough to accommodate three people, Kit was assisted by Midshipman Rogers-Tillstone and a boy seaman.

On arrival in my position I went rapidly through the usual drill, and in a few minutes reported to Lieutenant Commander Soutter in the foretop that the starboard battery was ready to open fire. I then had a look round. My outlook consisted of a slit in the armour about five inches deep, and about a yard across, allowing me to see from right ahead to fifty degrees abaft the beam, which was the arc on which the battery could fire. I at once saw the battlecruisers, who were about six miles away on our starboard bow, and two columns of three ships in each. As I watched they formed into a single line, at the same time altering course to the south-east and increasing to full speed. A few moments afterwards they opened fire – it was the most glorious sight, and I was tremendously thrilled. The leading ship [HMS Lion] fired first, and the others immediately followed – the flashes of the guns went all along the line very quickly. I could not see the enemy, who were on the far side of the battlecruisers, but I could see the splashes of their shells falling round our ships.

Both Tillstone and I were watching absolutely fascinated, and suddenly he said, 'Look at that'. I thought for an instant that the last ship in the line had fired all her guns at once, as there was a much bigger flame, but the flame grew and grew till it was about 300 feet high, and the whole ship was hidden in a dense cloud of yellow brown smoke. This cloud hung in the air for some minutes, and when it finally dispersed there was no sign of the ship. Although I did not know the order of the Battlecruiser Line, I had a feeling at the time that it was the 'Indefatigable' in which I had a very great friend, and I learnt afterwards that it was so.

Kit then lost sight of the battlecruisers, as the 5th Battle Squadron altered course to starboard in order to engage the enemy.

I heard the three ships ahead open fire, and it seemed as though we were never going to start firing ourselves – being the last in the line, we were naturally the last to get into range, but it seemed ages. However, we opened fire at 4.10pm on the battlecruiser 'Moltke' at a range of 23,800 yards. Owing to the great range, we fired slowly at first, and did not appear to be fired at in return, but after ten minutes or so some shells splashed down about 200 yards from the ship and I knew that we had got an 'opposite number' in the enemy line. It was at this time that the 'Queen Mary' blew up, but I did not see this, as our battlecruisers were now directly ahead of us.

The next thing I remember is seeing the battlecruisers, led by the 'Lion', pass close by us on the opposite course – they had sighted the High Seas Fleet and altered course 180 degrees away from the enemy to lead the German fleet towards the Grand Fleet, which was coming south from Scapa at full speed. Actually at the time I, of course, had no idea where the Grand Fleet was, and I don't think anyone else in the ship had either. The 'Lion's' centre turret had been badly hit and was out of action, and the guns were cocked up in the air at a very 'stupid looking' angle.

The German battlecruisers similarly altered course by 180 degrees, followed immediately afterwards by Kit's squadron, and both groups of ships followed the battlecruisers in a north-westerly direction.

This turn was an unpleasant affair, as we turned in succession and the Germans naturally concentrated their gun fire on the turning point. Moreover, we were the last in the line. 'Barham', 'Warspite' and 'Malaya' were all hit during this turn, and I think we should have suffered considerably if it had not been for the fact that the captain turned the ship slightly inside the wake of the other ships. As it was we were hit twice, both times on the armour, with no damage. This was my first experience of being hit. The whole ship seemed to jar, but I didn't notice the noise of the explosion to any particular extent. One might compare the sensation to the feeling in one's arms if one takes a sledge hammer and brings it down as hard as possible on an anvil, keeping one's arms rigid.

Incidentally, although the noise from the opening salvoes from the ship was terrific, after the first five rounds I didn't notice them at all, although we were firing solidly for nearly three hours, and the guns of 'B' turret were so close to my GCT that by stretching one's arm out through the slit one could almost touch them when they trained on the aftermost bearing.

The next hour and a half [4.50 – 6.20pm] was the hottest time we had. The battlecruisers and the two 5th Battle Squadron leading ships, 'Barham' and 'Valiant', were firing at the German battlecruisers and punished them very severely, while the 'Warspite' and 'Malaya' engaged the leading ships of the German High Seas Fleet. During this period, both 'Warspite' and 'Malaya' were heavily punished – 'Warspite' was hit in all 26 times, but had extraordinarily light casualties, only one officer and 13 men being killed. 'Malaya' was at first very lucky, and although shells were falling all round, and the ships deluged in spray, she wasn't hit much.

During this time the range of about 18,000 yards was still too great for *Malaya*'s 6-inch guns to be in action, and Kit therefore remained a spectator.

It was extraordinarily fascinating – the visibility was bad and it was difficult to see the German battleships distinctly, but one could see the flashes of their guns with great distinctness, and then after an interval of about 30 seconds the salvoes would fall round the ship. During this time we never had less than three ships firing at us and sometimes more. Ultimately two shells hit the ship simultaneously on the water line abreast the bridge – the whole ship shook with the shock and Lieutenant Commander Soutter called down the voice-pipe to ask if I was alright, and if the battery were alright. I called up the battery, and the cheery voice of Young assured us that they were alright there, and I told Soutter accordingly. But what had happened was that an oil fuel tank had been penetrated, and the fuel supply to 'A' boiler room cut off. The stoker in 'A' with great presence of mind realised what had happened, and switched over to another tank, but in the interval, brief though it was, our speed was reduced from 25 knots to 18, and the ship dropped astern. It is to be presumed that the Germans thought we were done for, for they opened a tremendous concentration of fire upon us. Captain Boyle estimated that at one time before we resumed our position in the line, we were being fired at by no less than seven of the enemy.

Immediately afterwards we were hit again by a shell which hit the upper deck above the starboard battery, penetrated and burst on No. 3 gun. My GCT was filled with fumes and blue smoke, and we were knocked backwards, but it cleared immediately and there was no damage. Soutter again called down from the foretop to know if I was alright, and I told him 'yes'. I put my face to the battery voice-pipe to enquire for them, but there was no need to ask, I could hear the most terrible pandemonium and the groans and cries of wounded men. Immediately afterwards I heard one man call out, 'Water, we're burning'.

At this moment, the Gunnery Lieutenant Commander called me through the tower voice-pipe and asked for information, and I told him I was afraid the battery was in a bad way, and asked for permission to go down and see what I could do. The only way down was by a ladder which led into the port battery, and on arrival there I found all the lights out, and a crowd of men who were having difficulty in joining up a hose to the fire main. This was soon put right, and then a Petty Officer said that the door at the forward end dividing the port battery from the starboard was jammed. I went forward to see and, as I expected, found that they had missed one of the clips in the darkness. While I was knocking this back the men with the hose just behind were playing it all over me, and I remember very distinctly using bad language at them about it. I only mention this because, when the door swung open, a big sheet of flame came through, and the fact of my being wet through probably saved me from being nastily burnt. Immediately afterwards five blackened figures rushed out – they were the survivors from No. 1 gun.

The German shell had burst on No. 3 gun, killing all its crew, and the explosion had set light to cordite on trolleys next to the guns. The flash of this swept fore and aft along the battery and caused immense damage. Of 121 crewmen, 104 were casualties. All the electrical circuits in that part of the ship were destroyed and the communication voice-pipes broken, while a huge fire started round No. 3 and No. 4 guns, which made it impossible to reach guns 2 and 5 and bring them into action.

The first person I saw in the battery was the gun-room steward, who had been laying the table for tea – these ratings usually form part of the Ammunition Supply Party or stretcher-bearers, or something like that. He was half burnt from head to foot – the right half of his hair, face, shirt and right trouser all gone, and seemed dazed, but walking and otherwise alright. He asked me where to go, and I gave him to a leading seaman to be taken to the Dressing Station – he died a few days afterwards. We got the fire under to a certain degree, and were able to pull a number of the wounded out, and I left the men from the port battery doing this and returned to the port battery myself, where I found McCulloch, who considered we would get at the fire best by getting through the ship's galley. We had some trouble with this door, which was a light one, and was badly jammed by the explosion, but eventually broke it down and got the hose through. I left McCulloch here and returned to the GCT where I reported to the Gunnery Commander. He replied that at all costs I must get as many guns going as possible, as the Germans were sending a destroyer attack down on us.

Kit had to use his initiative to get as many of the starboard 6-inch guns working as possible. No. 1 gun was working but lacked a crew, so men were transferred from the port battery to get it operational while an alternative system of control had to be established between No. 1 and No. 6 starboard guns to account for the destruction of the normal communication methods. Kit called No. 1 gun direct and gave orders, and they sent a messenger who ran across to a man in the port battery, through the aft door, and gave the orders to No. 6 gun.

When I returned to the GCT I found that the German destroyer attack had developed, and could see the boats coming towards us. I think that there were about nine of them. The attack was met by our gun fire, and also by the gun fire of some of our destroyers, who moved out from the rear of our line. Only one destroyer got within close range, although I think they all fired torpedoes. The one destroyer which came close got to within about 6,000 yards, and was received with an over-whelming fire, in which was included the two guns of my battery. Splashes were falling all around her like rain falling in a puddle of water. After about five minutes she was hit by several shells at once and sunk.

It was just about this time that I heard that the Grand Fleet were in sight, and a little later the 5th Battle Squadron altered course to port to make room for them as they deployed just ahead of us. We were still under concentrated gun fire from the German battleships, and for the last hour the visibility had been very bad, and at times the enemy were completely hidden in the haze. As we turned, a salvo fell in the water midway between us and the 'Warspite' and shortly before this we had received another direct hit on the roof of 'X' turret, which dented the roof right in but caused no casualties.

Once the battle fleet had deployed, *Malaya* altered back to its original course, with the 5th Battle Squadron then being at the rear end of the battle line.

The next thing I recollect is seeing the 'Warrior' and 'Defence'. These two cruisers were caught between the battle fleets, and came steaming down the line at full speed trying to get clear. They came under the most heavy concentration of fire, and presented a remarkable sight. 'Defence' was leading, both were belching smoke from all four funnels, and both were being repeatedly hit. Just as she came opposite us, and at a distance of about 3,000 yards the 'Defence' blew up. There was a huge sheet of flame, and then the awful pall of yellow smoke, and the ship was gone. There were no survivors.

Just as the 'Warrior' came abreast, I suddenly saw the 'Warspite', our next ahead, haul right out of the line and steam directly towards the enemy. She had been hit by a shell in the steering gear, and the ship was not under control. She thus interposed herself between the 'Warrior' and the German Fleet, and drew the gun fire on herself. It is an extraordinary thing she was not sunk – she was hit again and again, but managed to regain her position in our line. The 'Warrior' escaped, but was so badly hit that she sank at 10.20pm that night, after the survivors of the crew had been taken off.

The arrival of the Grand Fleet had an immediate effect on the amount of gun fire directed to ourselves. The 1st Battle Squadron were all firing away hard, the three which I could just see being the 'Marlborough', 'Agincourt' and 'Revenge'. Our bad time was over – from then onward we were scarcely under fire at all. Just about this time – I had lost all count of time, but it was actually at 7.00 – the 'Marlborough' was hit by a torpedo. Although almost right ahead of us I could just see her: she heeled right over to starboard, and I thought she was going, but in spite of this tremendous list she kept her place in the line.

The visibility at this time was very bad, but we continued firing intermittently for about an hour, after which the enemy were lost sight of, and a little later the order 'cease firing' was passed, and the gun crews fell out and had a bit of a stand-easy. I seized the opportunity of a quick run on deck to look at the hole where the shell had gone through into the battery, and then went down into the battery itself to help. By this time the fire had practically been got under, and the men were getting the wounded and dead away. The scene was awful, and is best left undescribed – poor Young and Cotton were both killed, and in most cases identification was only possible by means of the identity discs.

Kit used the brief respite to obtain some dry clothes and food. It was by then nearly dark, and as the battle had not been renewed, the ship's crew went to Night Action Stations. The night was pitch black and if firing broke out, as it did around 10pm, one could just witness flashes from shells bursting, but with little chance of telling who was firing or which side was which.

This particular attack took place about six miles from us, on our starboard bow. We could make out that there were about four ships on each side firing at each other, at apparently close range, and afterwards we learnt that it was Commodore Goodenough in the 'Southampton' with his squadron engaging some German cruisers. It was most spectacular – the vivid flashes of the guns, and the shells bursting made a fine sight. It went on for about ten minutes and then ceased – everything was black again, and one might have dreamt it all.

We saw several signs of fighting at a distance, and once there was a big explosion, but I don't know what these attacks were. We, ourselves, were not attacked at all during the night.

The only other excitement of the night was an attack which broke out about four miles from us, and almost astern of us, at about 12.45am. Firing suddenly broke out, and it was soon obvious that it was a destroyer attack on larger ships. The large ships were firing hard, and a few minutes later one destroyer blew up. Then a lot of guns fired together, and in the flash we saw that the large ships had cranes between the masts. I was on the bridge at this time, as this was my sight station, and there was a general cry of 'Hun'. The same flash illuminated the destroyers also – I could see them lying quite close to the Germans – the one which blew up was the Turbulent and, as I watched, the next in the line [HMS Petard] was badly hit. Immediately afterwards the leading German ship put a searchlight on us – it was only on us for a few seconds, but at once he altered course right round to port, and the whole line followed, and were lost to sight. I don't know to this day what ships they were. We certainly thought that they were battleships, but at night time everything is distorted in regard to size and distance, and they may have been the new cruisers, which also had cranes.

For the 5th Battle Squadron this was essentially the end of the battle, as the only remaining incidents experienced by Kit were of a minor nature.

The first was just after dawn broke (about 3.30am) when the whole horizon was clear, not a sign of an enemy anywhere, and suddenly out of the sky dropped a salvo of shell, about a mile from us. The Captain shouted, 'Where are they? Where are they?' We learnt much later that it was merely the 'Revenge' who, some fifteen miles away, had fired at a Zeppelin! The second was merely that just before we got back to Scapa on Friday evening – we were only a few miles from the land – the 'Iron Duke' suddenly opened fire, and several other ships followed suit. I jumped about a foot, but was told by the Gunnery Lieutenant that they were only emptying the shells from their loaded guns!

During the morning of Thursday June 1st, the fleet steamed about the battlefield in the hope of renewing the action, and we remained at action stations. We saw a certain amount of wreckage, but nothing else. When in the afternoon we set course for Scapa we fell out from action stations, and the men were fallen in and we mustered by the roll call. I read the muster for the forecastle division, to which I was attached – it was a grim business, and I was glad when it was done. I reported our number of casualties. At 8.00pm we buried 14 of the bodies who were mutilated beyond recognition. A short service was held and the bodies, sewn up in weighted hammocks, were committed to the sea.

During the day, and the following day, we were employed in cleaning up the battery – the whole place was a shambles, with twisted iron and steel everywhere, even after the debris was cleared up, and was not put right till the ship was refitted. The nose of the shell which dealt all this fearful destruction was found embedded in a tin of biscuits in the canteen. A large piece of the shell which penetrated the oil fuel tank was also found.

Our three doctors were wonderful. The terrible state of the wounded men made their task a very heavy one, and they were kept operating and bandaging for over 24 hours without ceasing. At the end of this time they were so overcome with sheer fatigue that the last cases were bandaged with the doctors lying down beside the patient, for they could stand no longer. Fortunately, the casualties which we had in the battery were our only casualties – none of the other hits which we received did other than damage to the ship herself. But even so, and not counting the ships which were sunk, the 'Malaya' had the second highest casualties of the fleet – the 'Lion' had the most, with 97 killed. HMS Malaya reached harbour on Friday evening, and the remaining dead bodies were buried at Lyness Cemetery the next day.

Jutland would prove to be the only major naval battle of the First World War. While the British suffered greater losses in terms of ships and casualties, the long-term result for them was a clear strategic victory. The German High Seas Fleet was no longer a viable naval threat and would make no further serious challenges to the Royal Navy, while the British Grand Fleet had retained their effectiveness and dominance of the seas. The German naval threat would remain, however, in the form of unrestricted submarine warfare in the North Atlantic, which resumed in 1917 and continued to intimidate merchant shipping throughout much of the rest of the war.

Kit Caslon (c. 1897–1973)

Following his naval service during the First World War, Kit rose through the ranks and followed a distinguished career in the Royal Navy. Serving as Captain throughout the Second World War, he acted as naval commander in March 1941 for Operation Claymore, the commando raid on the Lofoten Islands, and was Chief of Staff at Plymouth during 1943–44 where he commanded several destroyers including HMS *Somali* and the battleship HMS *Nelson*. Immediately following the war, he spent a year as ADC to HM King George VI and retired in August 1950 with the rank of Vice Admiral, having been awarded both the CB and CBE. Moving to Littlehampton in Sussex, he died in a nursing home in 1973 after a short illness, aged 76.

7 | Lawrence

THE BATTLE OF THE SOMME
JULY – NOVEMBER 1916

*Soon the wounded began to arrive: some
walking, some carried, some just helped along;
the usual bloody, patient, battered crowd*

Chantilly, located just over 20 miles from the centre of Paris and
surrounded by dense forest, played host to General Joffre's
headquarters. It would be here at the beginning of December 1915 that
the French Commander-in-Chief called a conference with his fellow
Allied leaders in order to establish a coordinated plan for the following
year's military offensives. 1916 was expected to be the year of the 'Big
Push', when a concerted effort from the British and French Armies
would break the deadlock of the Western Front and see the German
Army forced to give up the ground which it had been holding since the
end of 1914. A strategy of combined offensives by the British, French,
Italians and Russians was agreed upon for the following summer, with
an attack in the River Somme sector marked as the main contribution
by the British and French Armies. Following a major German attack
on Verdun in February 1916, however, the onus for the Somme shifted
more towards the British, as French troops were diverted to the Meuse
sector in order to counter the unexpected German assault.

The British soldiers who would be involved in the Battle of the
Somme included many from the Territorial Force as well as the
newly recruited volunteer Kitchener's Army. Among their number

was medical officer Captain Lawrence Gameson. Born in Walsall in April 1890 from a non-conformist background, Lawrence was an Oxford graduate and, at the outbreak of war, was studying medicine at the London Hospital. His father persuaded him against enlisting in favour of completing his medical studies, which he did in December 1915, and he was commissioned into the Royal Army Medical Corps at the end of the following month. He crossed to France in May 1916 to be attached to the 45th Field Ambulance, part of the 15th Division who were then based around Loos.

Planning for the Somme offensive continued throughout the spring of 1916, and by June the objectives of the battle were clear. The principal role in the offensive now belonged to the British, with their aim to inflict as many losses as possible on the Germans while relieving pressure against the French at Verdun. Rather than an outright victory, Haig's intention was to improve the British position so that their results could be exploited the following year. A five day artillery bombardment was intended to destroy the German front line defences, allowing an infantry assault to follow, which would be aided by a 'creeping' artillery barrage to prepare their way. The date of the infantry attack would be Saturday 1 July.

By the end of July 1916, when Lawrence Gameson's 15th Division began to move south to reinforce the Somme battle zone, the results of the offensive were already disappointing. Despite the British and French sending 27 infantry divisions into battle against the 16 German divisions, relatively little ground was captured. The initial Allied bombardment during the final days of June had alerted the German Army to the imminent attack, while in many places the shelling had failed to cut the enemy barbed wire defences or destroy the well-constructed and deep concrete German dugouts. Limited success was attained by the French troops advancing further south of the sector, perhaps because their attack followed after only a short artillery bombardment and so benefitted from the element of surprise, but along the main part of the British line the gains made

Lawrence Gameson, in a photograph taken
towards the end of the war

were minimal. The corresponding casualty rates were at a level
never previously experienced – the opening day of the battle alone,
Saturday 1 July, saw 57,470 British casualties overall, with 19,240
of them proving fatal.

By Friday 4 August, Captain Gameson had reached Levieville,
his unit's last halt before going into the line.

*The villages are increasingly neglected and dirty as we near the edge of
the Somme show proper. The countryside is packed with troops: troops
doing PT, bayonet drill, bombing practice, advancing in open order,
jumping in and out of trenches, even playing soccer in the shrivelling
sun. Cavalry are exercising. There are acres of camps under canvas,
obvious, scarcely camouflaged. Many prisoners' cages in the course of*

construction. A few occupied. All the roads are congested, shrouded in clouds of white chalky dust. Horse flies very troublesome this morning. Our march ended in a stiffish pull up on one of these so white roads. Got here at 9.30am. The tiny village is on relatively high ground; east it looks towards Albert, south it slopes to the valley of the Ancre.

Have just had my distant initiatory view of the battle-zone, I looked with the naked eye and then with field-glasses. In Albert I can see the church one has heard about; the gilded figure of the Virgin bent and toppling. A heavy bombardment, clearly visible, is going on far away to the east. It seems to be by our guns and the enemy's. Clouds of smoke and of chalk dust are hovering above the area. There are bright bursts of shrapnel shells in the air. It is all happening near some wood. When first I looked at this wood I took it to be the remains of an isolated industrial centre with clusters of chimney stacks still standing. It is a group of branchless tree trunks, more like a plantation of telegraph poles. The smoke hides it, blows away then hides it again as I watch. The whole landscape is so outside my ken that I feel I am not seeing France's living face but the nebulous country of dream life or an evil fairyland. But the landscape is very strange indeed, and yet more strange because of the orderly normality here and behind: a cool wind, a hot sun, wide reaches of waving corn. I can even see an old man threshing wheat with a flail, as I saw another in a barn this morning on the way here. Looking east once more I can pick out the white chalk trenches of enemy positions before the attack began.

The 45th Field Ambulance was to establish its headquarters in Fricourt, with their Advanced Dressing Station based in a ruined chateau in Contalmaison. It would be at the ADS that Lawrence would spend much of his time attending to the wounded.

We rode through Albert to the horse-lines, which are being established about a mile and a half behind Fricourt, and so on foot to this place. The dust pretty bad. Can chew it as you march. It sticks to the face thick as velvet and you need to look quite hard at a man to identify him. Sweat, trickling down the face, makes little runnels in it. I felt the heat a good deal. Fell out once to vomit by the roadside. The desolation is impressive: mine craters, blown-in trenches, sprawling barbed wire... and dust, dust, dust. Between Albert and Fricourt, now nothing more than a name on a board that's stuck on a post, there is seething activity. Troops are everywhere. Small valley after small valley crammed with transport; I counted thirty caterpillar tractors in one group alone. Masses of heavy artillery unconcealed in the open, dump after dump of war materials. In short, by far the largest military operation of the war and probably of any war ever. It is wholly impossible to describe either all this concentration of stuff or the newly made desolation surrounding it.

Our Main Dressing Station will be in Fricourt. Halted there to drop some of our party and then we slogged on to Peake Wood, a half-way post between Fricourt and Contalmaison. Not many people about. The region began to look nasty. From Peake Wood, downhill then up, to Contalmaison, which is quite completely ruined. We were told to turn left after the second bad smell. The directions proved to be as accurate as a precise map reference. Our party got here without incident. Hamilton is in charge of the ADS.

The Contalmaison dressing station was based beneath the remains of a chateau; a few chunks of wall and part of one room were all that was left above ground. Lawrence and his fellow officers inhabited the dugouts constructed many feet below the chateau's cellars, connected with the relatively fresh air outside by means of a long wood-lined shaft. Originally built by the Germans, the ventilation shaft now faced the enemy lines and so the new inhabitants were in constant fear of a shell falling down the chute and bursting in their small box room.

Already a shell has exploded almost on the edge of the opening. It sent down a great whoof of smoke, stink and dust which put out our lamp. Seems an odd place for living quarters; but I always tend to anticipate the worst. I am not always wrong. Here at Contalmaison I feel most curiously and disturbingly isolated, as if one is going to be stuck here for ever.

The following day, 11 August, would promise a baptism of fire.

Soon after breakfast, as Hamilton and I were dealing with cases in the cellars upstairs, a messenger dashed in with the news that Mametz Wood had been shelled. Hamilton sent Raymond forward to investigate. We were still dressing wounded when another runner arrived. He reported that a gas shell had burst inside our post in the wood and had poisoned the detachment. He further reported Raymond was hit. Hamilton went up, leaving me in charge of the chateau. Raymond was brought in with a buttock wound. He said a high explosive shell had done the damage. It had blocked the entrance, poured its fumes into the dugout and so fouled the post with carbon monoxide. I dealt with him and sent him to Fricourt.

Raymond had just left when the sergeant from the post was brought back. His stretcher was grounded outside; I thought at first glance he was asleep. He was dead. Next, word came back that Hamilton was unconscious. I put the ADS in charge of a senior NCO and went to collect him. Having gone, I suppose, about 50 yards I met Worthington, who had hurried on foot for the last part of the way from Fricourt and was out of breath. Gaily swinging his respirator by its strap and laughing his easy laugh he told me to return, said he'd go forward and went.

Our domestic troubles had caused work to pile up. Even the approaches were filled with stretchers waiting to be taken inside. The enemy chose this moment to shell us. I got all under cover, below ground or in trenches, but looking back from the entrance saw a German still on his stretcher by the main path. I was told he was 'supposed to be dead'. Such bland indifference totally unlike our men. Took out my informant to bloody well see for himself. The German was dead. Shelling had shortened by the time Hamilton was brought in, unconscious and frothing at the mouth. I sent him down by Ford ambulance.

Just as things were calming down at the Advanced Dressing Station, a runner arrived to report that Worthington, the officer who had volunteered to investigate the situation at the Mametz Wood medical post, had received a dose of the poisonous carbon monoxide gas which had infiltrated the wood.

I set out at once with a couple of men and a wheel-stretcher. As we neared Mametz Wood, Worthington came out from the trees. He had a branch in his hand for a walking stick and waved it in salute: odd after the report I'd received. Said all was now well at the post, but three of our men were dead. He ridiculed the stretcher, refused to get on it and sent it and our party to the post to bring in our dead. Could do nothing to persuade him; force was out of the question. He would not take my arm or accept any help. He was chatty, inclined to linger; just then there [it was] a very unhealthy place at which to linger.

On reaching the cutting we passed a few Jocks standing in the dugouts' entrances. [Worthington] showed unreasonable annoyance, flung away his stick and exclaimed, 'I won't be seen going lame by the blasted feet!' Now he was curiously, toxically elated. I did not know, and am quite sure he didn't, that carbon monoxide or, indeed, any product of an HE shell, could give rise to such alarming effects so long delayed. Anyhow, after discarding his stick he rapidly went limp. I took him without argument by a short cut over roughish ground. We got rather tied up in loose barbed wire, and involved in some tiresome shell-fire. I pulled him flat. He seemed lost to his surroundings and to what was going on. For the remaining distance to the chateau I dragged or partly carried him, unconscious. When I got him here he was oozing green frothy mucus. From a medical viewpoint it had been a bad journey. Of course it could largely have been avoided by using the wheel-stretcher.

This, as I've said, was out of the question without employing violence and physical restraint; neither of which appeared to be needed or justified when I first met him near our post. I took him myself by Ford to Fricourt, unconscious and a ghastly colour.

Journeys to the front line trenches were relatively unusual for a medical officer such as Lawrence, who spent much of his time based at the Contalmaison dressing station, with wounded and sick brought to him on a regular basis for treatment.

Albert, on the map to some at home, appears to be right in the thick of things. Here at Contalmaison, but a short way from the actual front trench, the latter gives one the impression of being remote. As far as I am concerned, it is. I know almost nothing of our immediate front, of what the infantry are doing or of their conditions.

Sunday 13 August brought good news regarding Lawrence's fellow officers, Worthington and Hamilton, who were both recovering from their recent gassing. Meanwhile, as the summer progressed so did the battle, with the occasional new attempt to advance being made but with few gains to show.

Still very hot. Early morning mist effects are the sole scraps of beauty in this filthy area. Today the sky is dotted with sausages, far more of ours than of theirs. The chateau and its grounds are being made into a strongpoint in case, we assume, the enemy counter-attacks in strength and attempts to get back lost ground. Large fatigue parties, mostly dismounted cavalry, are at work inside and out. It's a great nuisance having workmen in the house just now.

There is a continuous stream of wounded through at all hours. The pips on my tunic cuffs are shiny with polished blood, blood of someone else, of infantry mostly. Although but a middleman, one gets sick of blood's smell and of the endless everlasting procession of red raw human meat passing through our hands. We do not wear white overalls! Coats off often, and aprons.

This evening I killed 14 flies at one swipe with a rolled-up copy of an ancient 'Times'. They are infinitely numerous, leisurely and deliberate in movement and have large sticky feet; the neighbourhood is an incubator for them. Eggs are laid in the corpses of Germans and horses, hatching in the rotting semi-liquid flesh. The rest of their lives, for the most part, is an ephemeral gluttonish revel amongst all that is most revolting in this region of putrefaction and decay. They swarm upon our food, they buzz. Night and day this room resounds with their buzzing. The drone becomes a background. It even steals into one's sleep.

That night saw Lawrence undertake one of his rare excursions away from the dressing station. The infantry were making a concerted attack on a nearby trench and casualties were expected to be heavy.

We set up two posts between the regimental aid posts and here. My post was at the end of a short communication trench beside the road from the Cutting to Mametz Wood. I am vague about how far we were from the actual front line – in a state of flux I believe – well out of it anyway. I had Davies in my party along with a few men from the 46th Field Ambulance. On the way up, Davies told me that his normal job is on the tiny Ffestiniog Railway. He is very Welsh, a good NCO and a delightful fellow.

It is the first time I have been outside and directly in front of the guns when a barrage was screaming over one's head. The artillery have been active lately, but that is not at all the same thing. At zero the black sky was suddenly slashed by a semicircle of stabbing flames. The noise was prodigious, exasperating. I am told that one becomes used to it with practice, which clearly must be true. As the barrage eased and lifted we could hear the other din in front. Soon the wounded began to arrive: some walking, some carried, some just

helped along; the usual bloody, patient, battered crowd, without a
grouse and with scarcely a groan.

At about 4am orders came to withdraw to the chateau. It had been
an easy night. Our post was not shelled. The ground some 200 yards
to our left had been bumped solidly for about three hours, and the
road in front, as well I know, had had its share of enemy attention. I
do not know how the infantry fared – or how they stick it.

Despite the limited amount of ground taken by the Allies and the
drawn-out nature of the offensive, it was commonly believed that
the Germans were approaching the point of total exhaustion and
that the tide of the battle would turn. With a breakthrough expected
at any moment, the fighting thus raged on into September.

Throughout my stay at Contalmaison the flow of work in our cellars
was uncertain; times of slackness alternating with times of great stress,
when the place filled with scores upon scores of reeking, bleeding men.
Those times of great stress were not isolated incidents, to be dealt
with, cleaned up, then forgotten, like a railway accident. They recurred
regularly. They went on and on and on. Stretchers blocked the cellar
floors, the passages, the battered shelter that remained above ground
and the approaches outside. Often we worked for hours and hours on
end without respite: at the crude dressing-tables, at men grounded on
stretchers, at men squatting or sitting. It was emphatically not sheer
muddle, but the congestion beggars description.

Our working space was limited. We got in each other's way. There
was a constant movement of bearers shuffling and staggering with
stretchers, negotiating the cellar stairs, seeking a way in or out and
a bare space whereon to deposit their burdens. Walking wounded
sat on benches or squatted between the stretchers on each available
foot of floor, patiently waiting their turn to be dressed or to get their
shot of anti-tetanic serum. Sometimes a man on a stretcher would
vomit explosively, spewing over himself and his neighbours. I have

seen mounted troops brought in with liquid faeces oozing from the
unlaced legs of their breeches. Occasionally a man would gasp and
die as he lay on his stretcher. All this was routine; and the waiting
crowd looked on perforce. It looked on unconcerned. No one spoke
much during these seemingly endless periods of congestion. For the
most part, the wounded showed little reaction of elation or tendency
to talk and to exchange the customary quips. They waited patiently,
while we got on with our work with no needless words.

This was done in the poor light of candles and reeking lamps.
There was little water, and of course no running water. Dressings
and filth accumulated, to be burnt outside with the minimum of
smoke. The air became rank; worse when gas was about for airways
had to be partially blocked. Blood was the general background:
dried, drying or wet. With the means then available we did our best
for the wounded's immediate needs and for their rapid evacuation
by ambulance to Fricourt; and even that short journey was very
unpleasant when the enemy was shelling the roads or the chateau.

The dressing of undressed wounds and re-dressing of many, re-
splinting or splinting, removing or adjusting tourniquets, giving some
hot tea or food to suitable cases, the injection of ATS – and morphia
when necessary – then prompt evacuation to the rear, represented
roughly the limits of our helpfulness. We could cut away clothes,
but could seldom replace them; most went off clothed as they came
in, taking away much of their muck or dust. I am doing no more
than merely scratching the surface. The carnage of the Somme was
enormous. During the opening months the conditions were dreadful.

After a few weeks of recuperation, Worthington and Hamilton
returned back to the ADS, just in time to share Lawrence's first
direct experience of gas-shelling.

The bombardment was of phosgene, shrapnel and High Explosive,
a pretty usual mixture. HE and shrapnel were to injure personnel

and respirators, or to force men to cover (if any), in a trench or dugout, whither the heavier-than-air gas followed them. The ping and the vicious whine of the shrapnel bullets, along with the wha-wha-wha-wha-wha-wha-WOPP of the wobbling hesitant gas shells of liquid contents, are disquieting noises. Our anti-gas measures at the ADS were poor, so the cellars were soon filled with a sufficient concentration to be a menace. Fortunately we were slack; the cellars almost clear of wounded.

I regret that I must record how I made rather an ass of myself. Box-respirators of the early, crudish pattern had not been a general issue for long. I was uninstructed in the drill, which was quite different from that for the 'flannel hat' – the sticky flannel thing you just pulled over your head and stuffed into the top of your tunic. I nearly suffocated myself! I shouted to Hamilton that my specimen did not work. He told me (with pardonable impatience) that if I really had to suffocate myself, I must do it outside or in Hell. Anyway, he showed me how to adjust the thing; a relatively simple matter when once you knew the drill. It was a feeble start to a poorish night, for the shelling went on intermittently until dawn. The pattern of these respirators was modified later.

After some three weeks of concentrated work at the chateau, Lawrence was given a few days of rest in the nearby Fricourt. While still near enough to the front line, his billets were almost cosy in comparison to Contalmaison, with the mess being situated in a dry cellar lit by natural light during the day. Despite ostensibly resting, he still took a keen interest in the medical work going on around him.

As the Main Dressing Station of a Field Ambulance, our main job at Fricourt was the usual one of providing a link between the forward RAMC elements and the Casualty Clearing Stations in the rear. In one batch of wounded, I remember, there was a man with a loop of gut sticking out of a gash in his uniform. It was a bayonet wound.

The loop of gut had been lightly dressed with gauze, beneath which was a wriggling mass of maggots. The man had been lying out wounded, and the flies never missed a chance. His condition was deplorable. I gave him a hearty dose of morphia and let him be, going on with cases more likely to benefit from immediate evacuation. He improved beyond my expectation. I evacuated him later.

Save for the crumbled remains of the church, Fricourt had vanished. Its site was surrounded by the largest mine craters that had ever been blown. Debris choked the pond. An iridescent scum shone on the surface of the surviving puddle. I picked up a fragment of illuminated church music from the church's rubble. There was much heavy artillery about. An 8-inch battery was almost on top of our mess. The most fascinating piece was the 15-inch Howitzer; I often watched it firing. You could follow the shell nearly to the top of its trajectory.

At the end of the three days, Lawrence returned to Contalmaison and resumed his usual duties. By now he had spent more time at the chateau than any of the other medical officers in the 45th Field Ambulance, and as a consequence had seen more wounded men 'than one would have thought possible' in so short a time.

There was hardly a part of the body I did not see cut or exposed. Maggot invasion was common. I can recall an unconscious man who arrived with part of a frontal lobe protruding through a hole in his skull. The protruding portion of brain was moving with maggots. When men had had to be left out wounded for some time, often their shoulders, buttocks or whole back were invaded by the creatures in the areas of skin compressed by the weight of their immobilised bodies. One man I saw had been lying out because both his legs were wounded. Prolonged pressure had caused necrosis of the skin over his buttocks and of the superficial portions of muscle beneath it. Maggots had invaded the deeper tissues. I had to pick them out with long forceps. The man was unaware of his condition. Maggot invasion was always accompanied by a foul smell, since it flourished only in tissues undergoing some degree of decomposition. As a rule, the victim did not notice the stink, or did not know that it came from his own body if sensitive enough to notice it.

Apart from freakish bullet wounds, one saw what tolerably harmless tricks a bullet could play after it had entered the skin; for example, a lucky Jock. When his head had been tilted backwards, a bullet entered his tin hat between the lining and metal crown; coursed round inside of crown, then took a forward course from behind. It entered his shoulder and emerged below his collar-bone. Via his tin hat and him, it had described the better part of a circle without harming any vital structure.

Despite or perhaps because of stress caused by constant exposure to the suffering and tragedy implicit in such a major battle, Lawrence continued to exhibit a somewhat detached, professional interest in his medical work.

One slack day a corpse arrived. There was no evidence of the cause of death. This called for no enquiry, but I elected to do a post mortem. I staged the thing with care, and was just about to make the first sweeping incision when I noticed an unusual dimple at the side of the neck. It was the entrance hole of a bullet. There was no wound of exit. I had seen similar cases before; in the healthy skin of a youngster a bullet may leave but a tiny hole which closes at once. I clearly recall my chagrin as I replaced the amputation knife and declared the post mortem off.

Once I gave an anaesthetic while Hamilton completed the removal of a man's foot with scissors. I made a note of this, because it was the only anaesthetic I saw given at Contalmaison for all the hundreds of men we handled. Anatomically, I learned little from all I saw; yet, perhaps, I learned more than I realised. The work in our cellars was rudely done, but it was done with a singleness of purpose which is almost the sole refulgent and amending quality of medical men. The quality has precious little nobleness. It is a habit arising from rather hard training wherein all wasteful sentimentality is discouraged.

Rumours of a relief at last began to circulate, finally culminating in the arrival of one of the South Midland Field Ambulances to take up position at Contalmaison, allowing the 45th Field Ambulance to move out of the immediate battle zone on Monday 11 September.

We marched out in small parties, down the road to Fricourt, and so to horse-lines near Albert. Then we rode to Lavieville. We rode across open country, all out for part of the way. And what joy to discard the steel helmet, to feel the wind in your hair, to know again the thrill of unafraid movement.

Unfortunately, for Lawrence the promise of rest was to be short-lived. The following morning he received unexpected orders.

Worthington sent for me at 10am. He said that Broughton, the Medical Officer to 73rd Brigade Royal Field Artillery, was killed last night, that I must report to them for duty at once, and that I might take an ambulance to Peake Wood and then Brigade HQ. I've done all that and here I am in this dismal district again. Disappointing after yesterday's brighter prospects; besides, I feel rather mouldy, no doubt due to living underground at Contalmaison – but at last I am with a combatant unit.

I threw my kit on the side of the road near Peake Wood and eventually found 73rd Brigade HQ some 200 yards north of the road at this point; or rather, I found the Adjutant, the Orderly Officer and a few men knocking together a place for new headquarters. Fisher, the Adjutant, was doing most of the work. He is a short square-headed fellow with large hindquarters and a busy manner. He has an 'army' moustache.

When addressing you he gives the impression that he is cautioning you. He appears to have his own notions of welcoming the newcomer. Having told me how impossible it would be to find anyone good enough to follow my predecessor, he added, 'Poor old Doc got killed while cleaning his teeth, which is a damned silly thing to do in a place like this; and I hope you haven't been so bloody careless as to bring a toothbrush!' I think I shall like this Fisher man in spite of his odd manners, for he has pleasant twinkling eyes. Captain Graham is the battery commander. He strolled up to the battery just after we got there. He was carrying his tin hat, swinging it by the chin-strap. There was a splodge of white on it made, he explained, by a piece of chalk which had been flung at his head by the near burst of a shell. This appeared to amuse him. Already I feel more at home than ever I did with the Ambulance.

I have medical charge of 70th Brigade batteries as well as 73rd. I've been sent to live with their 'D' Battery which consists of four 4.5 Howitzers. I sleep here and am attached for rations. Have a cubby-hole of my own, so can scribble. It is in a bank between two 4.5 gun-pits. Smelly. Stretcher on floor for bed. Each neighbouring gun has been firing for the last hour. Every time a gun goes off the stretcher bounces from the floor. A wave of pressure shoves inwards my ear-drums. A strong, nauseous fireworky smell wafts in from outside. All this is new to me and one needs to get used to it. A queer feeling, however, lying inside my flea-bag flat on the stretcher in darkness, almost as immobile as the dead I have handled so often. Mawkish? It is. But this hole has a vault's smell, earthy. Walls are rotting planks. The floor is slimy with mud that stinks of the fields of death, of dung and of dead bodies. The guns are making my head ache. I can see now why this cubby-hole is going begging.

Now that he was based as an officer with a combatant unit, Lawrence enjoyed the privilege of a personal aide.

I have inherited a servant called Patience. He is also my medical orderly; my entire medical staff in fact. He speaks very slowly with a strong 'Brummagem' accent. He doesn't call me sir. He shows no sign of approval; or otherwise for that matter. I find the medical equipment has many shortages when checked with the lists of what I'm alleged to have taken over. I think that it may have been looted since Broughton's death. If this is so, then my Patience has connived at it. Such pilfering, or plain theft in peacetime, is regarded as reasonably fair play. It is covered by the generic term scrounging. I may be wronging Patience, yet he has an air of such unconcerned blamelessness that I wouldn't put it past him, not by a long way. I told him I would indent for replacements. He was not at all interested, dismissing the matter lightly with the irritating remark, 'What 'opes of getting any'.

Being in such close proximity to the guns was a startling new experience, and one to which Lawrence had to adapt at very short notice. Being attached to an active artillery unit, he was also more aware than before as to the course of the Somme campaign and the plans for new offensive actions.

Do these Gunners ever sleep? I have slept quite negligibly. My ears are buzzing. I am somewhat deaf. It is all very interesting, and I suppose I'll get used to the abominable noises in time

Much talk about an attack coming off tomorrow, in which the whole local front will engage. Much mystery about the 'TANKS' – secrecy hardly the word – we've heard much talk but no particulars. They go into action tomorrow for the first time, and this section is chosen for their debut. I know little of the infantry's programme. Although I now have a map, and can take a slightly more intelligent interest in the front, it tells me nothing whatever of the infantry's difficulties. Scores of guns firing together: quite near me are two batteries of 18 pounders, one of 60 pounds, an 8-inch Howitzer battery and our own 4.5's. An unexpected mixture to be huddled together. Flashes are spurting from hillsides and hollows; red, orange, white. The united noise is magnificent. Our line has been materially advanced since the 45th Field Ambulance was first at the chateau. Earlier, I heard the tanks moving up this road; the sound they make suggests a gigantic watch ticking. Shells are slithering and whining overhead. Mud is everywhere. Our lane is mud, its banks are mudbanks. Yet wild strawberries and brambles go on shoving up leaves to the light; pitiful patches of hopefulness. Men, horses, wagons, limbers and guns trample or tear up the earth making mud pies of the ground and green things.

Friday 15 September would mark a renewed British effort in the Somme campaign, with the opening of the Battle of Flers-Courcelette. A major attack was launched by 12 divisions across a 12 km front, with armoured tanks being used for the first time.

The attack has come off, after great activity and noise at the Gunners' end of the barrage. Few details have come my way so far, but batteries are moving into more forward positions. Done my round of all eight batteries. It has been a noisy day. Called at Contalmaison chateau and found a crush of wounded, ours pressing cigarettes on German prisoners. Examined a disabled tank. They did not do the dramatic things everyone had hoped; anyway, not on our Divisional front, from what little I can gather. They are presumably only in the experimental stage. Disillusionment about a magic wand to finish the war is nothing new. The infantry's unquenched optimism, or relatively unquenched, is frankly beyond me. I have just heard that our Jocks did exceedingly well: they took and held Martinpuich. The front is now fairly quiet.

The tanks had indeed been somewhat of a disappointment. Of the 49 vehicles intended to advance across no man's land towards the enemy, only 15 actually did so; the others had either broken down before reaching the front line or failed to start at the allotted hour. Yet the effect of the tanks on German morale was notable, and within the first three days of the battle, the British and Canadian troops had successfully advanced some two kilometres.

Lawrence's home with D Battery was not to last, as he was now detailed to the 73rd Brigade Headquarters, where he soon established himself after taking leave of his rough home with the guns. His new billets were much more pleasant, with the Headquarters mess situated in an old German shelter, dug out of the slope towards Contalmaison and well behind the Advanced Dressing Station in the chateau. Despite the improvement in living conditions, the facilities still left a lot to be desired.

Our bunks are infested with lice. Bishop contends they are German because they are field-grey in colour. We do not undress much, washing facilities are meagre, so I expect to become even more lousy. Though ignorant of what governs the matter, I do beyond question react more severely than most other officers to lice, fleas, horse-flies and blood-suckers generally; what's more, they seem to prefer me. At the entrance to our quarters a shelf has been cut to take our communal wash-basin. It is filthy. I have not yet begun to make suggestions. It appears that I am now permanently attached to the Gunners, so I'll wait until I am dug in. The formidable difficulties about cleanliness seem to be inadequately met. The Colonel does his ablutions in his own dark private hole.

Rather than taking sick parades at Headquarters, Lawrence preferred to visit the Brigade's individual batteries as a regular inspection routine.

Did the round with the Colonel this morning. He, too, hates noise. He was blown up earlier in the war and his ears were slightly damaged. Enemy anti-aircraft very active and much stuff zipped into the mud near us. At dinner tonight we had a near-miss by a 5.9; candles knocked over and place shaken, but no damage done. Colonel has been a bit touchy this evening. He observed during dinner that some of our linesmen had used obscene language when he was clearly within earshot. He decided quite suddenly to ring up their lair: 'What the Hell do you mean', he shouted, 'by using such foul language in

your Colonel's hearing? What's that? What's that? Pah! Mind it does
not happen again!' as he banged down the receiver.

I have just come in from a lone walk in the open. A heavy
bombardment is going on a little further north, near Thiepval
probably. Seems infinitely remote and no concern of ours. The smoke
has drifted into the valley below me. Through the haze of smoke and
evening mist I saw the higher ground on my left. Prongs of orange
flame stabbed the blue-grey haze. I watched the moon creep over the
mist into a dappled sky. I could smell hot oil and burnt cordite. I
caught the faint scent of mist, the faint scent of settling dew, which
maybe nothing can ever prevent or everlastingly sully.

Lawrence received orders on Monday 18 September that his Brigade
would enjoy a short period of rest, beginning the following day. The
Tuesday morning therefore saw him travel through Albert, the town
synonymous with the Somme which had been so visibly scarred by
the devastation from the on-going battle.

On the left, as you approach Albert, you pass the shattered Cemetery,
where the graves and the headstones are tumbled about. One solitary
figure remains on guard by an untouched grave. It is the only stone
figure in a cemetery which has at any time come near to pleasing
me. It stands there unscathed and white, head bowed, hands crossed
over breast. It stands quite close to the broken wall, quite close to
the traffic growling by in the road.

We passed a few civilians in Albert. They looked oddly out of
place in their own town. We met the 1st Division returning to the
line and we thought they looked rather under the weather. Groups of
kilted Canadian Scottish watched the Division march by. A military
band was playing in the streets. I know neither what band nor why it
was playing. Many of the houses are shaken, with broken windows
and damaged roofs; some are total ruins.

Our way led by the church and beneath the toppling Virgin. She holds the Child inverted above the street. I am quite untravelled, but have read a little, and I should think that this is the only monument in Christendom of Christ upside-down. It dominates the journey to and from the line on this part of the front. I will say no more, for I am well aware that moralizing about this gilded figure of Mary has been worn pretty threadbare by countless numbers of people. Countless numbers of people, however, do not as a rule moralize about the same matter without good cause.

We went by the Amiens road. A little way beyond the town we passed some German prisoners working on the roadside. The party, after the German manner, smartly saluted the Colonel. Which is not to say that our troops do not salute when working on the roadside, but that they are inclined to do so with a certain degree of bored condescension. Further along the road a small French girl came towards us. She held up her hand peremptorily. We halted. She was selling chocolate, which she had in a basket-tray slung from her slim shoulders. She demanded 1 franc per bar. The Colonel, assuming a manner evidently reserved for females, argued gracefully that the price was too high: 'Nous battons toujours pour la France!' ['We are fighting for France!'] he protested. 'If it comes to that', the child hit back, 'are not your *brave Allies fighting always for England?' We capitulated at once and paid her price. Solemnly the Colonel, I and our grooms urged on our horses. The child stepped aside. The Colonel saluted her.*

Returning at the beginning of October, Lawrence found that the front line had moved eastwards with the British advance. Their new headquarters were now at Bazentin-le-Petit, in the cellars of what had been the Curé's house, between a ruined church and Bazentin Wood. The newly captured ground was filled by the detritus of war.

Came back through Bazentin Wood. On the way there I examined an abandoned tank and took from it a damaged 6 pounder shell-case. The wood, a confused mass of living and riven trees, covers a large area. I lost my way in it. A hateful derelict place. Awkward going. I heard no bird, nor any soft scuttle of living creature. Everyone avoids it. I found German corpses and a fragment of German music. The tracks are blocked by fallen trees, cut by battered trenches; I had to climb over obstacles every few yards. It is tangled with half-hidden barbed wire. Twisted lines of a Hun light railway zigzag like snakes in and out of the brushwood. The brushwood is growing wildly. The fallen trees are sprouting from their flanks, a blind groping fruitless growth which is horrible. The whole area is horrible; and it preserves the likeness of a living wood. One of the many woods which were bitterly, bloodily contested. Still present there is the lingering stir of men's agonies. I was glad to be clear of it.

We are re-planning Headquarters. We have taken over the cellar next to the mess where the servants were. We have cleaned up for them a row of good German dugouts, but these quarters were not immediately well received. Half way down one of the stairways was a dead German. He had fallen head foremost and was stuck there. On my preliminary examination in the dim light I could see only his field boots. I had come without my torch. Subsequently, on looking closer, I found that his flesh was moving with maggots. More precisely, I noticed that portions of his uniform were heaving up and down at points where they touched the seething mass below. The smell was pretty awful. None of the men would touch him, although troops as a rule are not noticeably fastidious. The job was unanimously voted to me, because it's supposed, quite wrongly, that doctors don't mind. I went down the stairway with a length of telephone wire and lashed it round the poor chap's feet. We hauled him up and dragged him away for some distance. The corpse left behind it a trail of wriggling, sightless maggots, which recalled the trail in a paper chase. Having moulded a shell hole as grave, we erected a board at the man's head: 'An Unknown German Soldier', with date of burial. All identification marks had gone. We hoped that they had been officially noted by his friends or our people; but the Hun had pulled out in a hurry from here, and our lot had had scant opportunity. There are still many dead lying about.

Further success in the Somme campaign was marked by the capture of the village of Le Sars, north east of Martinpuich, news of which reached Lawrence on 8 October. The Brigade's batteries moved forward yet again to maintain their distance to the advancing front line. Once more, the captured ground was full of many dead soldiers from both sides.

We walked to le Sars, the north-east edge of which was virtually our front line. The old German trenches west of the village were crammed with German dead. Some of them had their tongues stuck out and almost severed by their teeth. The eyes of many were sealed with mud. They were mostly quite young men. It was all pretty grim, for they lay on their backs or their bellies in distorted postures of uncomforted agonies. The stink was revolting. I got into one trench to examine them more closely. I removed several buttons and shoulder-straps.

We left these trenches and scrambled into the south-west corner of the flattened village. Some caution was needed because Brassey did not know just how our front line ran. In the village we found the body of a British soldier, not of our Division, unburied and decomposing. His identification discs were somewhat defaced. These and his pay-book I posted to the base. I copied some of the letters I found on him before sending them and other papers, with a few exceptions, to his wife; who, one might say in passing, would have raised no objection. Indeed, this little dossier has an intrinsic value that marks it out for keeping. I should be sorry to have lost the letter from his mother:

> Dear Son John, Just a few lines for your birthday. I have just been reading thy letter on to myself… I would like to post you a nice present but am getting a pair of stockings knit for thou. John, meny a cry when I lay down for thou. I am such a bad letter writer. So no more. Short and sweet. God be with us till we meet again. Love and meny kisses. Mother.

It was not meagre sentimentality which urged me to take copies of these letters. Something more fundamental was concerned. They seemed to be wholly appropriate. They were the stuff of raw human sorrow, a very tiny fragment of the sum of suffering. In John's left breast-pocket was a photograph of his young daughter. I kept it, because both pocket and picture were torn by the piece of shell or bullet which clearly had killed him. In a letter with the photograph his wife calls John Jeffrey, which is nobody's business but theirs:

> Jeffrey, God knows I have many a weary night and day for I never go to sleep but I see you somewhere or I am talking to you for my mind is so much upset for it is now we know how we love each other but we will just have to hope for the best and trust you will come safely through it all. May God send you safely through this terrible war safe, from your own dear Annie. Good night.

To the emotionally costive or immature these letters may seem of small comfort to the man who received them. They who wrote them knew better. The letters were quite untouched by deceit, like so many others written then.

We covered John's body with bits of turf, with plaster from the houses and with the ends of broken bricks. As I lay in the dark that night on the damp floor of our cellar, I wondered what in God's name must the grand total be of ours and the enemy's – if this one man had three generations of women to mourn him.

This single British casualty which Lawrence Gameson buried in a crude grave was only one of many, many thousands of soldiers killed during the summer and autumn of 1916. If one battle summed up the First World War, it would be the Somme. A small amount of ground was taken, but at an incredibly high cost. The opening day alone became legendary, with the great hope of an extended artillery barrage and widespread infantry assault resulting in the highest casualty rate of any day in British military history. By the official end of the battle on 18 November, when the wintery weather began to set in and any further continuation of the campaign became pointless, the overall British casualty figures had reached 419,654, of which 131,000 were dead. French casualty numbers had reached 204,253 while the German Army had suffered between 450,000 and 600,000 casualties. The sacrifice in individual lives was appalling and lessons would be learned. But sadly an end to the war was not yet in sight.

Lawrence Gameson (1890–1972)

Lawrence was demobilised in January 1920. He became house surgeon and anaesthetist to a provincial hospital for six months before joining a Devonshire medical practice in Okehampton. Marrying in 1921, during the following years Lawrence and his wife had three children while he honed his skills as a General Practitioner. They moved to Bath in 1938 where, at the outbreak of the Second World War, he helped to run one of the city's main First Aid posts. From 1943 he spent a rewarding period as medical officer to a large mental hospital outside Hull, and finally retired with his wife to a cottage in Somerset in 1957 where he spent his days writing poetry, playing the piano and gardening. In a preface to his memoir written in 1958, Lawrence wondered whether the document 'may not at last come to rest in some museum or junk-heap'. It was therefore in line with his wishes (or at least the first of them) that the account ended up in the archive of the Imperial War Museum in 1978, where it remains one of the collection's finest accounts of the Somme. He died peacefully at home in 1972, aged 82.

8 | Bobby

WAR WORK
AND THE HOME FRONT

*Then suddenly up came the searchlights and there
was the Zep, so low you could see the cars hanging
underneath and almost over our heads it seemed*

Gabrielle West, known as Bobby to her friends, was 24 years old at the outbreak of war and lived with her parents in the village of Selsley in Gloucestershire. Her father was the local vicar, and she helped to run the parish Sunday school. As supporters of the local branch of the British Red Cross Society, Bobby and her mother contributed to the town's war work by accommodating Belgian refugees and, in their capacity as members of the Voluntary Aid Detachment (VAD), from spring 1915 had cooked and cleaned at the Red Cross Auxiliary Hospital in nearby Standish. The VAD had been founded shortly before the war and, closely associated with the Red Cross and Order of St John, was a popular organisation among middle- and upper-class women who were keen to contribute directly to the nursing and care of their nation's soldiery.

Despite the support received from her parents, the voluntary nature of Bobby's work was soon causing her financial difficulties and so she began to look for a paid post, eventually accepting an offer from Lady Lawrence's Munition Makers Canteen Committee to run a canteen for the workers at the Royal Aircraft Factory at Farnborough. For a salary of £60 per annum and two meals a day, she was to cook for the mainly female workforce. Accompanied by her small dog, Rip, Bobby set out for Hampshire on Saturday 8 January 1916 in order to meet Miss Buckpitt, the Canteen Committee's representative, at her new lodgings near to the factory.

Not a very cheerful outlook when I first arrived. Did a melancholy three miles peddling through the mud, with Rip tailing disconsolately behind. Several airplanes flew low across the road and each time Rip squatted flat in the road petrified and refused to come on. As the road was full of traffic it gave me several bad spasms.

At last I arrived at 'Ye Olde Farme House', as it is called, and was told Miss B had not been able to meet me, but would I go down to the factory to see her. Here I was met at the gates by an armed sentry who refused flatly to let me in. I went round to the other gate and was held up by a policeman. Returned to first gate and found a bakers cart also trying frantically to get to 'the new canteen'. We were told there was no new canteen, and we ought to have passes and he wasn't going to let strange people into the factory, etc. However by the simple process of just 'remaining' until he got tired of the look of us, we were let in. Then I had to find the canteen. No one had ever heard of it and it was rather like hunting a needle in a haystack. Well after a bit I arrived at the end of a long series of planks which led across a huge morass to a wee little wooden hut, but there was no Miss Buckpitt so I had to go away and come back later.

This time I found a very forlorn looking figure sitting on a box in the empty canteen, no table, no chairs, pots or pans, no cupboards or shelves, only three tiny gas stoves, Miss Buckpitt and the box and at the far end two men slowly and solemnly washing the floor. They had only one bucket, one piece of soap and one flannel between them so their progress was not exactly rapid. The equipment was supposed to be on the road, so we sat and waited for its arrival. It turned up at about 7.30 and we worked like slaves the rest of the evening till nearly 10, unpacking it and putting it in order. As the canteen was to open on Monday there wasn't much time to waste.

The following day was spent at the canteen preparing food and getting ready for the grand opening on Monday. With cupboards and shelves quickly constructed and linoleum laid, the empty barrack room was swiftly converted into a plausible kitchen and mess room.

Farnborough itself is a beastly place. It consists of one long ribbon of mud designated 'the main road'. At one end are the shops, at the other are our rooms and about halfway between the factory. The shops don't bear talking about. The country round is very pretty, pine trees, heather and rhododendrons rather like Bournemouth, but the roads are perfectly vile, cut to bits by the motor transport waggons. Also large tracts of country are covered by barracks, ranges, etc., so that if one does not know one's way, one may walk for miles through about a foot of mud in the most desolate country, nothing but gas works, waste land and army buildings. But to anyone not used to it, the flying and the soldiers are most exciting. There are nearly always from two to ten to twelve aeroplanes up, some of them looping the loop, doing the most wonderful spirals, banking, etc. Sometimes they swing first their 'heads' up and then their 'tails' up, then go along in waves or shoot straight up and come down in a spiral, so straight that the inside wing is over practically the same spot all the time. We once started to walk across a large flat field when an aeroplane landed and began scuttling straight for us – my word did we run. Being chased by a bull is bad but an aeroplane is ten times the size and has six times the pace, it's horrid!

On the Aldershot road there is a continual procession of soldiers – first a train of mule waggons, then a military band, then 20 or 30 guns, each drawn by six horses, then a detachment of cavalry, then horses out for exercise, then a little squad of Flying Corps men, then a string of motor transports, then a whole camp moving quarters, baggage waggons, field kitchens, and all the rest of it, frightfully exciting.

Monday brought Bobby's first day of proper canteen work.

[We] found that there was hardly any gas pressure, so that it took hours to get the potatoes to boil and it seemed almost impossible to get the meat to roast. And if you light more than two of the five comic little stoves, they all go out. However, things did get done somehow but we only sold about six plates of meat and no pudding. At tea we had rather more to do but not a great deal, but still, we don't feel a bit discouraged; naturally they sent out scouts at first to spy out the land, and if they only take back a favourable report I hope the others will soon follow.

After a few days at Farnborough, Bobby felt that she could begin to distinguish the different characters of worker whom she served in the canteen. The vast majority were female, the absence of men who had enlisted to fight having provided women with an opportunity to undertake work for which, in peace time, they would rarely have been considered suitable.

Most of the girls are quite nice and quiet. We have about a dozen clerks who come down before the general dinner hour. They are rather haughty, but not so bad. The others are ordinary factory girls from various departments of the factory. There are the 'Welders' who join the metal parts of the planes by means of strong acetylene blow lamps. These give out such dazzling sparks and flames that they have to wear dark blue, almost black goggles. They also wear blue linen overalls and caps. Then there are the 'Dope' girls. They varnish the planes with fast drying, very poisonous varnish. It affects the liver, therefore the girls thus employed are under medical supervision, have to drink large quantities of lime juice and lemonade, must not eat in the dope room, must wash before meals, etc. But the majority are 'Cody's girls'. Mr Cody is the foreman of the 'shop' where the planes are covered with linen. He is the son of the Cody who invented the biplane and was eventually killed in an aeroplane accident. His uncle was Buffalo Bill. He is an awful little bounder but quite amiable.

There is one girl, and luckily only one, who is the most accomplished little cheat I have ever met. Nearly every day she devises some new scheme for 'doing us down', and as the voluntary workers are constantly changing and are, some of them, not over bright in any case, she very often succeeds. The first time she gave me 1/- or 2/6d for a 1d cup of tea, received change from one worker, went away and presently came back to another worker and vowed she'd not yet been given her change. Next day she gave me seven halfpennies for something worth 4d – in the scrimmage of serving dinners it very nearly got overlooked. When this no longer worked, she devised the plan of buying a cup of tea, carrying it to a distant table and, coming back, would ask for the loan of the milk jug a minute as the tea was so hot. Then she drinks the tea, refills the cup with milk and returns the half empty jug, at no charge. Of course no one but these silly old volunteers would allow the milk to be carted off this way. She really is so ingenious I can't help having a sneaking admiration for her.

Bobby soon took exception to the voluntary workers at Farnborough (despite having worked for some while herself in an unpaid capacity), who she felt were often unsuited to their jobs.

Really voluntary workers are the limit. About eight out of ten are married women and yet there is only one out of the whole lot who knows the barest elements of cookery and housekeeping, and there are not more than half a dozen with even a glimmer of common sense. There are two very dashing young ladies who come sometimes, they are covered with paint and powder and smoke cigarettes, etc. I set them to peel potatoes and onions and they were frightfully delighted, attacked the job with shrieks and chuckles of glee. I remarked to one of the other workers that they seemed to be having a high time over it and she smiled and remarked, 'Well you see, I don't suppose they have ever done that sort of job before. They are the nieces of the Duchess of Wellington'.

With her supervisor Miss Buckpitt having left Farnborough at the end of February, Bobby was notionally in charge of the canteen and anxious that the new operation should succeed. Accounts for their first full month were calculated on the first day of March, with positive results.

Out of £56 takings we have paid out £8.5s, in salaries £8.4s and made a clear profit of £14. That is really very good, as it means a profit of 25% so I feel rather bucked. Although these canteens are started by society ladies as a sort of contribution to the war, they are not supposed to be charities but are expected to pay back the money advanced for equipment, and after that to make enough so that when the war ends they can be kept on with paid instead of voluntary help. Any extra profits will be put to charitable uses. A very good scheme I consider. Much better than pauperising people who are earning record wages and are quite able to pay fair prices for good value.

Time spent at work at the factory was interspersed with walks through the Hampshire countryside, accompanied by her canine companion.

I started out to Bagshot Heath. The road was ankle deep in mud, fearful soupy stuff. On each side were barracks and stretches of mud dugouts and trenches. Every now and then you come on a row of ghastly 'corpses' swinging in the wind, awful bloated sacks with straw sticking out of the 'bayonet wounds'. Every few yards a waggon or motor transport passed and spattered mud right up to one's neck. All the time there was a thin drizzle falling, so it was thoroughly jolly and festive. Rip pattered along at my heels grunting and puffing with rage when he got splashed or met with an extra formidable puddle. We paddled along like this for about five miles, getting more and more depressed until at last we got to Chobham Ridges, which is really quite interesting. From there we went into a corner of Bagshot Heath. Neither is at its best in winter, being rather black and dismal, but it is quite romantic. In the mist and wind and drizzle it made me think of Beau Brocade [a popular historical romance from 1907 by Baroness Orczy, better known for The Scarlet Pimpernel] and Dick Turpin and all the tales of people robbed and murdered and highwaymen hung in chains and creaking corpses in the wind. But five miles through mud in a drizzle isn't very inspiring. Quite refreshing after the deadly monotony of Farnborough.

Miss Buckpitt returned on 13 March with some exciting news.

The Committee sent her down to ask me if I would accept the job of caterer to the new canteen at Woolwich. There are various points in its favour. In the first place I am very dull at Farnborough and as Miss B is to be at least four months at Woolwich so as to open seven new canteens, I shall see a good deal of her if I go there. Then there is to be a rise from 25/- a week to 34/- which will make all the difference. 25/- is a fearful squeeze when rooms and laundry and everything else is so dear. Thirdly it is a distinct promotion, as Woolwich is a much larger canteen than Farnborough. So I have accepted and am to go on Monday next.

Eager to start her new post but fearing that it all seemed too good to be true, Bobby travelled south the following week, staying at her brother's flat in London before arriving at Woolwich to begin night duty on 22 March. She found her new location very different from Farnborough.

Woolwich is of course a slummy part of London. In fact there are slums all the way between here and London which is one and a half hours by tram. But it is rather amusing for all that. Beresford Square outside the main gate is a big market full of coster's barrows, fruit, vegetables, fish, tripe, winkles, flowers, knives and tools, livestock and all the various wares you see at Petticoat Lane. There are also street jugglers, palmists, etc. performing. All along the road to the Arsenal are weird little shops.

There is also a sort of crèche for pipes and baccy. The work people are not allowed to take their smoking outfit into the Arsenal, so for a few pence a week they can leave them just outside the gate. Imagine Oxford Street with no pavements and no islands but with a railway running down each side and the road a sea of mud and rubbish and you will have an idea of what the 'Long Straight' at Woolwich is like. You leap out of the way of a motor lorry and land under a train, bundle out from there and run full tilt into a swearing navvy who wants to know by all that's holy why you can't look where you are going. It's the limit.

The canteen is between the danger buildings and the firing pits, so by day the noise from the guns is tremendous, cups leap off the shelves and every now and again a window breaks, but luckily I am spared that at night. We serve a lot of boys with buns, sweets, oranges, tea, mineral waters, etc. all through the night, also a few men. Then we give dinners to a lot of girls and some men at 11.30. At 3.30 tea for the girls, at 4.00 tea for the boys, at 5.30 more boys and a lot of men so that we are busy the whole night except 12.30 – 3.00 when we have our own meal, scrub all the tables, etc. It is pretty strenuous, far more exciting than Farnborough! We take from £4 to £5 every night and by day they get £12 – £15. When you remember that nearly all of it comes in in coppers it means a good deal of work.

The girls are very rough, regular cockneys, mostly very nice and amiable, but if one does happen to get roused it is just Billingsgate gone mad. If they are aggressive the only thing is to be equally so and to give them as good as you get, they generally shut up and become quite meek when they see you are unabashed by their abuse. One of them attacked me today because she had to wait a minute or two for her dinner. We were short of helpers and were going as hard as ever we could so I whipped round and said, 'Well how many pairs of hands do you think I've got? Six?' She looked quite abashed and shut up at once.

Some of them come from the fuse shop, but a good many from the danger buildings. This is where they fill the cartridges, etc. for bombs. They have no end of rules and regulations. When they arrive they have to go to a barrier, take off their shoes, jump over the barrier in stockinged feet and put on slippers on the other side, for fear of any grit coming in on their shoes. They also are not allowed any hair pins, so wear their hair down their backs in plaits, and also they must not wear any metal buttons, etc. on their clothes.

It was not long before Bobby experienced the 'frightful thrill' already familiar to those living in and around the capital city. The night of Saturday 1 April brought her first experience of an air raid.

We had not been long in the canteen before the foreman came butting around adjusting the curtains, etc. and it began to dawn on me that we were in for a raid. 'I'll send some of the boys over to get something to eat', he remarked, so for about twenty minutes we were busy serving buns, tea, coffee, mineral waters, etc. Just as the last boy was served, out went the lights. As soon as the lights go out each foreman is supposed to lock the door of his shop. This is a necessary precaution because one could not have hundreds of panicky men and women charging about in the dark in the open. Some of the girls in the shops near started to squeal and then began to sing, but the boys were absolutely quiet. There wasn't a sound except the policemen whistling to each other and the foreman and watchman calling.

Then all of a sudden the guns began. They don't make a great noise, only a sharp short bang almost like revolver shot. Of course the big naval guns make a deafening noise, but they did not fire them tonight. I made tracks for the door in hope of seeing. The Zep was just about three miles up like a small sausage in the sky, very high up. The minute it came into sight, three searchlights were playing on it and the guns opened fire. It was hit three times. Each time it lurched and then gave a bound. Then it rose higher still in the air, turned round and did an ignominious bolt. The whole performance was over in five minutes. As the Zep retreated it began dropping bombs. These landed partly in the river, one or two in North Woolwich where they destroyed two or three small houses and killed several people and the rest in fields and open ground where no damage was done. Obviously the Zep was badly hit as she came down very low and seemed lopsided as she disappeared and made an effort to get home before she collapsed, but failed, for in the morning there was great rejoicing at the news that she had come down in the Thames.

Meanwhile, Bobby and her companions sat in the cold darkness, waiting for the 'all clear'.

It got very cold as the radiators were turned off, so we lit the ovens and sat in front of them with the doors open. There were only four of us, the Cook, the Char, the old watchman and myself. The watchman is the weirdest old bird. The very fattest, stupidest old thing you ever saw. He is exactly like a tortoise; he has not only got the face of one, but also the figure and just about the brain power. He talks in slow gasps, with long wheezing pauses between like an old person who has just woken out of a nightmare and he often spends the whole night from 7pm to 6am asleep in front of the radiator, except that he occasionally rouses himself sufficiently to eat a little food in the torpid sort of way that a tortoise eats dandelions I suppose he thought it was his duty to try and cheer and encourage us poor females so he roused himself from his hibernation and remarked: 'Last time we had a raid, I did have a dreadful time I did. When the lights went out, the cook was here and "Oh", she says, "You wicked man", she sez, "To turn out the light", she sez, "You wicked man". And she takes hold of my coat she does and I thought she would have hit me she looked so savage, and the char woman there! She hung onto my arm and cry! My word did she cry! And I says to them, "My good women", I sez, "It ain't my fault", I sez, but it wasn't a bit of use, they kept on just the same.' The thought of that poor old reptile besieged on one side by a frantic cook and on the other by a tearful char was so funny that I simply roared, until the tortoise slowly turned his head towards me and remarked, 'Zeppelins weren't no laughing matter' in his opinion. After that I felt rebuked and subsided.

After this he regaled us with spicy reminiscences of the wreck of the 'Princess Alice' (a pleasure steamer that was rammed and went down with all on board somewhere near here). He especially dwelt on the rows of corpses in the mortuary and other pleasing aspects of the tragedy. It all happened thirty years ago. Well we managed to while away the rest of the night fairly comfortably, what with frequent meals and long snoozes, and the 'Princess Alice' until about 3.30. The lights came up again and in five minutes in came a whole hoard of girls, men and boys all clamouring for dinner. Of course none of the volunteers had turned up, so I and the cook had to do everything with the char in the background. Luckily the boiled beef and carrots were cooking before the lights went out, but there was of course no pudding.

A strategic bombing campaign by the Germans against England had commenced in January 1915, largely delivered through the use of Zeppelin airships and, later, Gotha aircraft. Although damage to military targets was minimal, one of the main purposes of the bombing campaign was to affect civilian morale, and in this respect it was successful. Until more effective aerial defences were established towards the end of the war, Zeppelins were considered as a deadly threat by the civilian population and, especially following the German use of chemical warfare during the Second Battle of Ypres, the possibility that they might choose to drop asphyxiating bombs on British towns developed into a definite fear. Bobby and her colleagues had already been temporarily issued with gas masks in case the threat materialised, but the watchman had forgotten to ask Bobby to return hers.

Nasty little black gauze things. I found out after that they are no use unless wetted. As they were given out in little oil silk parcels in the pitch dark, I don't suppose anyone could have found their way into them in

time even if the Zep had dropped any numbers of 'stink bombs'. I am
frightfully proud of mine. Fancy having a real live respirator!

The frustrations of daily work helped Bobby to forget many of the
larger issues of the conflict, yet throughout the year the Zeppelin
threat was ever present to remind the population that the war was
on their very doorsteps.

No end of Zep excitements lately. A few weeks ago we heard distant
guns in the middle of the night and then some hours later, more guns,
still a long way off. We waited a few minutes and then went into the
road. There was a funny whirring noise which we took to be the
motors that carry round the anti-aircraft guns. There was no firing
and no searchlights. Then suddenly up came the searchlights and
there was the Zep so low you could see the cars hanging underneath
and almost over our heads it seemed. We just turned and scooted.
There was a tremendous din of firing and then we heard a number
of big bangs and a great smell of smoke and things began to patter
on the roof. My word, were we scared. We stood in the kitchen
not daring to breathe and heard the whirring noise go right over
our heads. When we ventured out to look, the beast was making
off towards the Thames having passed right over the hutments. I
thought I really was dead that time.

The next morning on our way to work we passed three villas
completely wrecked and every window all down the street was
smashed. Seven people were killed. These houses were only about
200 yards from the hut so no wonder we were scared. A lot more
damage was done and several more killed at Greenwich and other
places. No one knows exactly why, but certainly there was something
wrong for the searchlights to let her get so low before lighting up and
giving the guns a chance. Some say a German spy put the leading
searchlight out of action (i.e. the one the others have to follow),
others that the officers in charge all went to a dance and others that

the men who work the searchlights got drunk. You can believe what you like but certainly something was wrong somewhere.

Following this scare, many Arsenal workers including Bobby and Miss Buckpitt (or 'Buckie' as Bobby now affectionately called her) received four days of leave in place of many postponed bank holidays.

We went to Deal and had a jolly time. It is a dear old place. The beach is full of trenches, barbed wire and dugouts. When it rained we went and sat in one. Out at sea is a little fleet of destroyers who search each boat that goes up or down the channel. You see the destroyers in the middle and a little row of steamers on each side meekly waiting to be searched.

Returning home on the Sunday evening ready to start work on Monday, Bobby retired for the night only to be awoken almost immediately by the sound of gunfire.

We went out and saw a Zep far away to the south. I used to think a Zep raid rather exciting but since the last I feel I've had quite enough. Instead of feeling pleasantly thrilled I just feel squirmy inside and very cold and clammy. However it disappeared and the firing ceased. In about two hours it began again, so again we trotted out but could see nothing. All this time we had been sitting in the cottage drinking tea and discussing the war with our neighbour's family and our neighbour's neighbour's family. We were just going back to our own hut when we heard wild cheering and saw the whole sky turn red and then we saw the Zep in flames to the north. She just came floating gently down until a big piece of burning stuff fell off and then she nosedived to the earth and it was all dark again except for two little red lights twirling madly about where she fell. I never heard such a noise in my life. All the hooters in the Arsenal and on the barges yelled at once and all the workers in the Arsenal roared and shrieked. All the boys in the YMCA hostel up the road sang 'Tipperary' and all the neighbours scuttled about congratulating each other. Even staid, respectable Buckie and I danced around each other and crowed.

Later we heard that the twirling red lights were Robinson and another airman doing a sort of war dance of loops and spirals over their enemy's remains. [On the night of 2 September 1916, Lieutenant William Leefe Robinson became the first British pilot to shoot down a Zeppelin over Britain, resulting in his award of the Victoria Cross for the action.] This was the Cuffley Zep. A few days later we saw the second one come down at Potters Bar and not long after that the third. Of course there were others brought down but not in flames and so of course they were not visible from a distance. Although all these were some distance from Woolwich (the first one being in fact on the other side of London) they appeared quite close, say about 10 or 12 miles away. We had half a mind to start off to see it, only we had to be up so early the next morning.

Returning to the daily chores of the factory canteen, Bobby's problems with her volunteer workers continued as the year progressed.

Am getting rather fed up. Last week two of my women didn't turn up. On Wednesday the cashier was taken suddenly ill. The Committee undertook to send new workers. On the following Monday two very beautiful ladies arrived from the London Office and informed me I was to employ them at £1 a week. Of course I didn't want two such duchesses, what I wanted was one cashier and three washers up. However I shifted the staff around a bit and put one in as cashier and the other as night head. In about a week all sorts of rumours and scandals were afloat, and one morning I found the following chalked on the door.

SMOKING CONCERTS HELD HERE EVERY NIGHT
ALL GENTLEMEN CORDIALLY INVITED
BUT BE SURE & LEAVE YOUR WIVES BEHIND

So the two lovely ladies had to be hustled off in double quick time. Apparently no enquiries had been made and no references taken up when they were engaged by the Hon Sec in London. The result was I was left two short and as it was the fault of the Committee for sending such creatures I asked them to find me new ones. No one came for over a week, then a very pretty, feeble little person of sixteen who of course is going to be more trouble than she is worth.

The stresses of running the canteen with unsuitable staff soon mounted up and by the beginning of November, both Bobby and Buckie had had enough.

Have escaped from Woolwich at last! The dirt and the noise and dirty swearing people were beginning to get on my nerves a bit. Buckie has got rooms in London and I am staying at [her sister] Joan's flat and we are both looking for work. It is the funniest (most odd) thing in the world being an out-of-worker. We have interviewed one artistic diaphanous lady with a view to becoming housemaid and cook respectively. She offered £40 and £30 per annum and all she wanted was to have good cooking and no trouble, didn't mention whether she would care to have the house kept clean or not, probably not. We didn't sign on. Next I saw an advert for girls to drive Lyons bread carts and sell their bread and cakes, so I went and was interviewed by a fat porpoise of a man and two skinny little men who sat in a row and goggled at me. I was not found suitable but was asked if I would like to be a seater in the restaurant at a salary of £1 a week. Didn't know what a seater was so I stuck my nose in the air and said £1 wasn't enough. He said there were plenty of chances of advancement. I still sniffed. Then he asked what money I had been taking and I said 35/- and my board and made or tried to make a dignified exit. After this we rubbed at several other jobs such as another canteen at Darlington, housekeeper and cook at Bristol Infirmary, the same at a girl's school in Studley, and so on.
Then we heard that Women Police were badly needed so went to their offices to see what that was like. All the WPs we saw were very

smart in a very dapper uniform of navy blue. We were interviewed by an Inspector who was very nice and discovered the following details. They are anxious to get WPs recognised as an official branch of the men's police to specially deal with women and children. So far they haven't had recognition for their work, only a sort of 'toleration', but certain county and borough councils have employed WPs on their own responsibility, paying them out of local rates and taxes. They work independently of the men police and are not sworn in. Also a few county police associations have done the same and in a few cases they have actually sworn them in like the men. But the government (i.e. Ministry of Munitions) have recognised them and employed them largely inside factories to control the women workers and this is what they want recruits for. Pay is £2 a week which isn't bad but recruits have to buy their own uniform. They have taken up our references and if we are accepted I think we shall go alright, it sounds nice.

Just a few days later, both women were accepted as new recruits and summoned to begin their police training. There were about 20 other trainees, most being ladies of 'a much better class' in Bobby's opinion. Training lasted a fortnight and consisted of lectures, attending courts in order to take notes, and evening patrols. The patrolling was with a Women's Police sergeant at night and was concentrated around Victoria station and other 'lively' neighbourhoods. Other training was undertaken around Paddington, where two policewomen were employed by the District Council in order to help schoolchildren cross the roads and prevent them entering public houses, while reporting broken steps or railings and generally patrolling the streets. Bobby and Buckie's initial posting was to a factory at Chester, where they arrived on 20 December 1916.

The factory is about five miles from Chester and you go by train. On the morning shift you have to rise at 4. Horrid! Still, you get the afternoon to yourself, and as the work is not too hard you aren't too exhausted to enjoy yourself, as at Woolwich. The work consists of the following duties – searching incoming workers for matches, cigarettes, spirits, etc. in pockets, baskets, etc; searching outgoing workers for stolen property; keeping guard at the gate and allowing no one to enter without a pass; conducting stray visitors round and dealing with new workers, lost passes, lost clock cards, etc.; keeping order in the clocking shed; keeping the office where clerks, etc. sign on and off, enquiries are made, etc.; patrolling to see that no one is larking or slacking. We take turns at all these various jobs, none of which were taught us during training. We have two hours off for meals, so life is not too strenuous. Chester is a lovely old town of half-timbered houses, a fine Cathedral, a very interesting old church and also a complete city wall you can walk all the way round, about three miles. The river is good for boating, so in the summer I shall try and learn how to row properly.

A week later, both women were clearly doing well at their jobs, having already been promoted: Buckie to Sub Inspector and Bobby to Sergeant. Both were reassigned to a munitions factory near Pembrey in South Wales on 8 January.

For patrolling purposes the factory was divided into areas, with the room where Sulphuric was converted into Nitric acid and Nitric changed into Oleum being the most unpleasant. Here the air is filled with white fumes and yellow fumes and brown fumes. The particles of acid land on your face and make you nearly mad with a feeling like pins and needles, only more so, and they land on your clothes and make brown spots all over them, and they rot your hankies so that they come back from the laundry in rags and they get up your nose and down your throat and into your eyes so that you are blind and speechless by the time you escape. All over the place there are to cheer you on your way notices telling you what to do

Bobby West (back row, second left) in the uniform
of the Women's Police

*if anyone swallows brown fumes: 'If concerned give an emotic. If
blue in the face, apply artificial respiration and if necessary oxygen.'
Being quite sure you have swallowed numberless brown fumes,
this is distinctly cheering. Each time you leave you feel like Dante
returning from Hell.*

The town of Pembrey where Bobby resided was quite remote, being
a little coal-mining village with a small harbour and the remains of
what was once a silver works. The munitions factory was three and
a half miles from the town and, according to Bobby, built in 'the
most desolate spot in this world'. The factory sheds were constructed
amongst sand-hills, as for safety reasons the most dangerous work
had to be done underground.

The girls here are very rough, so are the conditions. The language is sometimes too terrible. But they are also very impressionable, quite friendly one minute and shrieking with rage and almost ready to tear one to pieces the next. One of our duties here is to get the girls out of their dining halls and back to their sheds at the proper times. When Buckie and I and the three constables first attempted this they merely hooted and booed at us and when we tried to insist, they all went on strike and assembled on a sand hill and announced that they would down the first constable who came near them. However Buckie and I marched boldly amongst them, much to their amazement and commenced to hold forth, 'telling them all about it'. By and by one or two cried out to the others to 'shut up. They've got a bit of pluck anyhow', and after one and a half hours of argument and entreaty they went back. They have never been so naughty since.

I find these girls here much more interesting than those at Chester. They are so full of life and cheerful and there are so many 'characters' amongst them and a great many different types. Of course there is a huge number, 800 in one section and about 500 in other sections in each shift, making a total of 3,900 women workers. Some of these are girls from lonely little sheep farms in the mountains, these speak only Welsh or a very little broken English and are very good sorts, though rough. Then there are the wives and other relatives of the miners, from the Rhondda valley and other coal pits near. They are very full of socialistic theories and are perpetually getting up strikes in true Tonypandy style. [A series of violent confrontations between striking coal miners and police took place in south Wales during 1910 and 1911, collectively known as the Tonypandy Riots.] But although so violent, when they think they are being trampled on they are very easily influenced by a little oratory and as soon as they have made up their minds 'to go back' they become as meek as lambs, if you spout at them long enough.

Munitions factories were full of danger, not only in terms of the explosive nature of the material involved in arms production, but also with regard to its effect on the workers' health.

The ether in the cordite affects some of the girls. It gives them headaches, hysteria and sometimes makes them unconscious. If a worker has the least tendency to epilepsy, even if it has never shown itself before, the ether will bring it on. There are about 15 or 20 girls who sometimes get these epileptic fits, and on a heavy windless night as many as 30 girls will be overcome by the fumes in one way or another. By rights, girls who show signs of epilepsy when put to work on the cordite ought to be transferred or dismissed at once, for if this is not done they become confirmed epileptics and go on having fits even when not in contact with the fumes. However this is not done and some of them have as many as twelve fits, one after another. When these girls get taken ill, we are generally called in to render what assistance we can and to take them up to the surgery on a stretcher. There are only three beds there and so if these are full we do the best we can to make them comfortable in the dining rooms. In this way we have begun to win the confidence of the girls and some who were most aggressive in their attitude towards the Women Police are beginning to get quite friendly.

There is one girl here, Mary Morgan, who gets the most appalling fits. She goes dead and stupid for a minute and then very red in the face and then starts the most violent struggles, pulling at her own hair, scratching her own face and twisting herself into the most fearful contortions. It takes four or five to hold her down and prevent her from harming herself. The favourite 'cures' among the girls is to souse the sufferer with cold water, thump and slap her, shake her, pour hot tea between her teeth (although being unconscious she can't swallow), stand her on her head (when she is purple in the face already) and last but not least sit on her 'stummick'. This particular girl told me after her last fit that she was so glad the Police Women had looked after her and kept the other girls away as last time she was that bruised in her inside that it made her sick for a week.

Considering the nature of the work being carried out at munitions factories, it was perhaps inevitable that every so often, disasters did occur. The morning of Tuesday 3 April brought particular excitement to the Pembrey factory.

Such a day! At about six o'clock there was a tremendous explosion and then a whole succession of little bangs. I rushed upstairs and from the window saw flames and smoke rising in volumes. The landlady wept and wailed and said we should all be killed and that poor Miss Buckpitt was certainly already dead and the poor women police and all the girls blown to atoms. I flew into my uniform with the old girl clinging round my neck and bolted off to the bicycle shop. There I hired a bike (my own of course was punctured just when I wanted it). When I got near the factory I met several girls running for their lives. One of them stopped me to say she had left her case containing her food in the dining room, would I please be sure to go and rescue it as soon as I arrived at the factory! When I did arrive I found the Danger Gates barred and all the girls huddled just inside them. A large shed behind the Gun Cotton section was in flames and going off in small explosions every now and then. All the police women on duty were busy pacifying the girls and attending to various cases of fainting and fits. After about half an hour of this performance the fire was put out and we were told to get the girls back to their sheds. This was easier said than done. However after another half an hour of persuasion one girl announced she was going back and she hoped if she perished the policewomen would remember that she had left all her money to her mother, we should find the will under the drawing room carpet.

Despite the obvious danger from accidental explosions, some munitions workers at the factory could be remarkably lackadaisical when it came to following the established safety regulations.

The girls here and the men for that matter are very troublesome about bringing matches and cigarettes. A week or two ago one of the

Women Police actually caught a girl smoking just outside a danger building. Last week a girl just going off duty came to the Police Office and asked me to please rescue her coat from one of the danger buildings, as she hadn't time to go back for it and catch her train. She told me I could recognise the coat because her pay slip was in the pocket. When I went for it I found the pockets full of cigarettes! Of course the poor wretch had to be prosecuted, though it was obviously an oversight or she would not have sent me for the coat.

. This factory is very badly equipped as regard the welfare of the girls. The changing rooms are fearfully crowded, long troughs are provided instead of wash basins and there is always a scarcity of soap and towels. The girls' danger clothes are often horribly dirty and in rags; many of the outdoor workers, who should have top boots, oilskins and sou'westers haven't them. Although the fumes often mean 16 or 18 casualties a night, there are only four beds in the surgery for men and women and they are all in the same room. There is another large surgery but it is so far from the girls' section of the factory that unless it is a serious case girls are not taken there. There are no drains owing to the ground being below sea level; the result is a horrid smelly swamp. There were until recently no lights in the lavatories and as these same lavatories are generally full of rats and often very dirty, the girls are afraid to go in.

Bobby and Buckie were destined to move jobs yet again in May 1917, this time to a shell-filling factory in Hereford. There they found that the discontent which had existed among the workforce at Pembrey was even more prevalent, with regular bouts of industrial disputes and general disgruntlement at the working conditions.

The girls here are really rough and very unruly simply because they always get their own way and they know it. Endless rules are made and we have to enforce them. The girls strike and go and yell outside the main office for an hour or two. The manager or his assistant comes

*out, hears their grievance and says it shall be removed and it is. They
promptly find a new one. Strikes and rows are more sport than filling
shells. We have already had half a dozen strikes which all ended in
the same way. Two shifting women dismissed – strike – reinstated.
Three girls dismissed for laziness – strike – reinstated. Girls wish for
a rise – strike – rise given. Girls object to being controlled during
their dinner hour or when they leave the plant – strike – now they do
what they want. It is therefore almost impossible to keep any sort of
order, because they know they will not be punished for disobeying.*

The final week of August 1917 was a particularly difficult one
for Bobby. Relations between English and Irish workers had been
particularly strained since the Easter Rising in April the previous
year, and with girls from all backgrounds mixing in the factory, it
seemed inevitable that trouble would result.

*Some time ago several lots of Irish girls were taken on. There
had been a lot of bad blood between them and the English. The
Irish sang Sinn Fein songs and made offensive remarks about the
Tommies; the English replied in kind. Each side waxed very wroth.
This went on for weeks and Buckie reported to the manager that
trouble was brewing. Last week during the dinner hour an English
girl accused an Irish girl of stealing her dinner. The Irish girl replied
by spitting in the English girl's face. There was a battle, all the others
standing around and cheering on the combatants. We were called in
to separate them. We had to lock the Irish girl up in our office as the
others wanted to lynch her.*

*Next evening, scenting trouble, eight or nine of us went down to
see the shift train off from Hereford station. A tremendous battle
ensued on the platform between about twenty Irish and the rest of
the shift. We got the Irish separated out one at a time and put in the
waiting room. I stood guard in front of the door, which unfortunately
wouldn't shut. Behind me stormed the Irish and in front the English,*

*until the latter were gradually pushed across to the other platform
and got into the train. Then we let the Irish girls out. They insisted
on walking at once to the factory to see the manager, so we walked
with them. Crowds of people hooted and threw mud at them; one
girl fell and was kicked by a young man in the crowd. I and another
WP grabbed him and called a policeman who had seen it done but
instead of taking him the policeman slunk off, so we had to let the
man go. Arrived at the factory and the girls were taken to see the
manager. All shrieked at once, but in the end it was settled that they
should all be sent back to Ireland the following day. Meanwhile we
attended to the injured. There was a broken head, several cuts and a
lot of bruises and a strained wrist. Next morning the Irish girls were
put into reserved carriages and sent off to Ireland. The Herefordians
assembled on the embankments and pelted the train with rotten
vegetables, eggs and bad language. So ended the Irish rebellion.*

Despite the occasional stand against misbehaviour, Bobby became
increasingly disappointed at the failure of the factory management
to address the frequent strikes which plagued work at Hereford. It
did not help that some of the male police stationed at the factory
were dismissive of their female colleagues.

*The Superintendent of the Specials employed in the factory is a little
cad, always ready to catch us out, and make fools of us. He was
just the same under the previous WP Inspector. He came into our
office one day without knocking and began to bully, rag and sneer
at me about some report I'd sent in. Persisted in calling me 'My dear
Lassie'. I told him he was a nasty little cad and if he called me that
again I'd throw him out of the office. He seemed vastly tickled as he
is a tall man and about twice my size. However he was standing near
the door, as when he called me 'Lassie' again I gave him a sudden
shove and banged the door up against him with my other hand and
landed him outside before he knew it. Later I went down and gave a*

*report of my deed. They began to solemnly put down a long report
of the incident, but relapsed into giggles half way through so I don't
think I shall get into very serious trouble for my breach of discipline.*

By September 1917, events had escalated to the point where both
Bobby and Buckie had reached the limit of their patience. Despite
being in positions of authority within the factory, as Women Police
they lacked many of the powers available to their male counterparts.

*For some time Buckie has been trying to get away from Hereford.
The Picric acid makes her ill and she has had several gastric
attacks. Also it is rather disheartening to work under a manager
who is constantly inventing new rules for us to enforce, but does
not back us up by punishing those who disobey them. But the real
reason is that B has been fighting to get us sworn in. In a factory
like this where we have a good deal of genuine police work to do
(i.e. prosecuting for bringing in matches, for theft, blackmail, etc.
and our work during strikes and riots) it is really important that
we should have the power to take out and serve a summons and
carry through a case without being obliged to pass everything over
to the men police. As an instance of the importance of being sworn
in, during the strike the girls attacked a police man and knocked off
his helmet and also knocked down a police woman. For assaulting
the police they were liable to six months hard labour. Assaulting
the policewoman counted only as common assault, as we, not being
sworn in, count as private individuals and the maximum penalty is
one month.*

Buckie in particular was a strong advocate of equal rights for women
officers. Ultimately, both she and Bobby would find themselves in a
stronger position of authority at other munitions factories, including
the Royal Gunpowder and Small Arms Factories at Waltham Abbey,
where they would serve for the rest of the war with the Women's

Police. While the conflict had provided women with an important opportunity to engage in areas of work which until recently had been the sole domain of men, there remained discrepancies in levels of pay and authority which would persist for many years to come.

Bobby West (1890–1990)

Bobby's grandfather was Dr Charles West, the founder of the Hospital for Sick Children at Great Ormond Street in 1852. She wrote her diaries partly for the benefit of her absent brother, Michael West, who during the First World War was a colonial educator based in India who went on to pioneer teaching English as a foreign language. Following the disbandment of the Women's Police at the end of the war, Bobby ran a tea shop in Chepstow in the 1920s which proved a success. Never marrying, she spent much of her life caring for various aged relatives and finally retired herself to a small cottage in Swanage, Dorset, which she shared with her assortment of small dogs. Bobby died in 1990, having reached her 100th birthday.

9 | Bert

THE THIRD BATTLE OF YPRES
JULY – NOVEMBER 1917

Hundreds of guns suddenly belched forth their projectiles and the air above us became filled with shrieking, screaming, droning shells

Following consistent failures to turn the bogged-down trench warfare of the Western Front into a war of movement, Allied conferences in November 1916 and the spring of 1917 led to the formulation of a new strategy. The Nivelle Offensive – opening on 16 April 1917 and named after the French Commander-in-Chief Robert Nivelle – saw a joint French and British attack on Arras and the Chemin des Dames ridge, intended to be the turning point of the war. However, despite the Allies capturing the greatest amount of ground since the war began, the extremely high casualties sustained by the French Army in particular were not enough to break the German resistance. Mutinies among the French halted any further significant gains and led to the sacking of Nivelle in May 1917, and his replacement by Philippe Pétain.

A campaign in Flanders was intended to follow the spring offensive, with the British in particular being keen to force the Germans out of Belgium and thus liberate the strategically important coastline. The last major battle in this area had been the Second Battle of Ypres in May 1915, since when the front line had been relatively static. A preliminary attack was launched at Messines on 7 June 1917 which successfully removed the Germans from the high ground to the south of the Ypres Salient, while the main British effort was reserved for 31 July, when the campaign proper would begin in the Salient itself.

Destined to play a role in the battle was Albert Atkins, who had enlisted at Hornsey in September 1914 just a few months after his 16th birthday. Despite his parents consenting to his joining up, he was obliged to lie about his age in order to be accepted and claimed that he had just turned 18. After the standard period of military training in the 2/7th Battalion Middlesex Regiment, which transformed him and his fellow recruits 'from pale civilians into hale and healthy soldiers', Bert was sent in February 1915 to Gibraltar for garrison duty. This relatively safe posting was not to last, however, as in July that year he was chosen as one of a draft sent as reinforcements to the 1/7th Battalion and saw action on the Western Front, ultimately as part of the support troops for the Battle of the Somme in July 1916 (during which his unit suffered heavy losses).

In August 1916 it was discovered that Bert had enlisted under age, and he was sent down to the base at Etaples. The harsh military training and uncomfortable life at the camp were not to his taste, and he was grateful to be sent home in October to join the 7th (Reserve) Battalion at Tunbridge Wells. However, boredom soon set in and he remained keen to return to the fighting. In June 1917 he answered a call for volunteers to join the Machine Gun Corps and, after training at Clipstone in Nottinghamshire, he crossed to France again in August 1917 at the age of 19.

A few weeks before Bert's return to the Western Front, the Third Battle of Ypres had begun. At 3.50am on Tuesday 31 July, a creeping artillery barrage was started to accompany the advance of the British, French, Australian and New Zealand infantry into no man's land. Initial results were promising, as substantial ground was captured and significant casualties inflicted on the Germans – although the attack by the British II Corps across the Gheluvelt Plateau to the south of the salient was met squarely by the main body of the German defence, and floundered. The weather proved to be a crucial factor in the battle, as heavy rain began to fall on 31 July and continued throughout the coming weeks, leading to the already devastated ground, churned up by constant artillery fire, turning into a boggy sea of mud and preventing any easy advance.

Bert and his fellow draft were initially based at the Machine Gun Corps headquarters at Camiers, during which time they were inoculated and went through the usual military training routine of gas chambers, bombing and gun drill. Glad for the opportunity to be sent nearer the action, Bert volunteered for a draft to the 198th Machine Gun Company, based with the 58th Division, and on Wednesday 26 September he marched to Etaples and entrained. After a tedious and uncomfortable journey in cattle trucks, they arrived in Belgium at Proven and marched to a rest camp at Houtkerque, where they stayed for the night in large marquee tents.

Next morning a motor lorry took us to Reigersberg Camp, just behind Ypres, where we joined the 198 Machine Gun Company. Whilst at the camp, which was composed of bell tents with no sandbag protection, we had a bad time with shells and every night regularly the Bosche would be overhead with his load of bombs, hurling death and destruction in all directions, but although he appeared to make a special target of our little camp, we were lucky enough to have very few casualties. As the company had just been through a 'stunt' at Ypres, we went back for a rest, and on the evening of October 1st 1917 we marched to the railhead at Vlamertinghe to entrain. Whilst waiting for the train, over came a squadron of German planes and began dropping bombs all round the station. This lasted for some time and things became so serious that we had to take refuge in shell holes of which there were hundreds close to the railway lines. When things quietened down a little and the planes began to disappear, we boarded the train of cattle trucks about 9.30pm but as soon as the train began to move, over came another flight of Hun planes and bombed us for about 15 kilometres down the line. Of course the

Bert Atkins in a studio photograph, dated
March 1916

anti-aircraft guns were busy, but the only thing they did was to make
a few more shrapnel holes in the woodwork of the trucks in which
we were trying to snatch a little sleep.

Arriving at the small village of Clerques, the men were billeted
in a dilapidated barn. They managed to cover the gaping holes
in the roof and walls with large pieces of sacking and sandbags,
although the constant rain meant that they were unable to avoid
getting drenched. On Saturday 20 October, the 198th Machine Gun
Company entrained for the Ypres Salient and Poperinghe, where
they arrived early the next morning and were billeted in a large
empty house in the town. The following day, Bert was surprised
to find his name listed for a promotion: 'so I henceforth held the
exalted rank of Lance Corporal'.

On the 28th, we made yet another move forward to a collection of huts just behind the line, known as Kempton Park. A more desolate wilderness is hard to imagine, unless it is the area two or three kilometres further north east, in which scattered shell holes, filled with water, mud and men, constituted the front line. On arrival at Kempton Park we sorted ourselves out into huts (which were about 15 yards long and 6 yards wide and the walls and roof of which were formed by bow-shaped corrugated iron), one section in each hut, so that by the time we had got our guns, tripods and accessories in as well, there was no room to spare. However, we took off our boots and prepared for a welcome rest. But we had not been down long when an order was issued stating that a certain number of NCOs and men were to proceed at once to the front line at Passchendaele in readiness to go over the top at sunrise next morning. By the way, the word 'sunrise' in this case was simply another way of saying dawn, for we saw no sun for weeks. Nothing but rain, mud, desolation and then some more rain!

I was picked to go as one of the NCOs and somewhere about 1.30am saw our party leave the others and after clambering over barbed wire in the dark, slopping through liquid mud up to our knees and slipping into shell-holes and tripping over duckboards, we eventually arrived at a trench-board track which we followed. As we tramped along in single file, sweating under our loads (for we carried full marching order with guns, tripods, ammunition, rations and cans of water) we continually passed doubled-up heaps that had once been men, but who now had fallen foul of one of those flying death-dealing lumps of shrapnel or machine gun bullets, and had passed to the Great Beyond. As we continued our way I, and no doubt each one of us, was thinking of home and wondering whether we should ever see it again, or should we come to the same fate as those poor fellows we had just passed? But it was part of our job to think only of the task we had in hand and to keep our minds from wondering about the future.

This attack would prove to be the final assault on Passchendaele Ridge. Having begun on Friday 26 October, the aim of the attack was finally to capture the small town of Passchendaele and the ridge upon which it was located. This higher ground was deemed to be of strategic importance, especially as in the coming winter months it would prove a much better position than the lower, muddy areas of the salient.

The most terrible thing about this Passchendaele front was the fact that when a man got wounded he stood practically no chance of survival at all and simply sank into the liquid mud and was drowned. I saw stretcher bearers making herculean efforts to save wounded men from this end, but in vain. It was impossible to carry a man on a stretcher, being knee deep in the mud. I even saw one of these stretcher bearers lay a badly wounded man on a sheet of corrugated iron and struggle to drag him over the mud on that. But it was hopeless and after a short distance, the corrugated iron and the man both sank out of sight. Those stretcher bearers were real heroes in endeavouring to carry out such a hopeless and heartrending task.

Following the carefully laid wooden boards across the morass of mud, Bert and his machine gun section arrived at their destination which proved to be an old German pillbox at the end of the duck board track.

This was in front of Passchendaele Ridge, at Poelcapelle. At least, that is where Poelcapelle had been, but there was no sign of it now. It had evidently been blasted out of existence and swallowed up by the mud and water. Incidentally, on our way up, I noticed a post stuck in the mud on which was a notice stating 'This is Wulvergem'. Obviously this was another village which had completely disappeared. Anyway, we dumped our gun kit and sat down in the mud outside the pillbox to wait for our barrage to open to clear the way for our advance. We waited here for about four hours in the pouring rain and every few minutes Jerry sent over shells, high explosives and shrapnel. One shell dropped clean in the middle of us killing three of our number and wounding about seven or eight. Once more I was lucky! The wounded were dressed with our field dressings and taken to the nearest dressing station and the other poor fellows were buried and their graves marked by rifles being stuck in the ground, attached to which were pieces of cardboard with the names, numbers and regiment of the men. No doubt, later on, these rough graves were found and proper crosses erected to mark the sacred spot.

At last, just as the sky began to lighten in the east, a loud boom sounded somewhere behind our lines and a few seconds later, a huge shell rumbled and droned overhead, to drop with a crash on an enemy stronghold probably several kilometres away. This was the signal for our barrage to open and as if by magic, hundreds of guns suddenly belched forth their projectiles and the air above us became filled with shrieking, screaming, droning shells, each one of which dropped somewhere in the midst of the enemy, churning up the mud, blowing up barbed wire into the air, smashing pillboxes, destroying and mutilating the enemy and his works. We had our four machine guns mounted with the sights set at a pre-determined range and were pumping out bullets at the rate of 600 to 700 a minute. Belt after belt we fired, hoping that our bullets were finding billets among the enemy. At last, the terrific din subsided somewhat and we had the order to cease fire, and we advanced just behind the infantry.

This was the secondary phase of the battle, intended to gain a base for the infantry to launch its final assault on the ridge. Bert received orders to take his gun team to a pillbox which had just been captured and establish a defensive position there.

On arrival we found that the Germans had been completely driven out, and I mounted the gun outside with spare ammunition ready to repel any counter attack which could be expected. However, things gradually quietened down, and later on another gun team arrived with our officer, Captain Reid, in charge. He told us to go inside the pillbox for a rest, leaving two sentries of the newly arrived gun team to keep a look out. After a small tot of rum and some bully beef and biscuits I was detailed to take my team (numbering now only five men) to a certain place to fetch a gun, tripod, spare parts, ammunition, etc. which had somehow been left behind in the melee by another team. So we started out through the mud and in the dark, picking our way past certain ruined objects such as splintered tree stumps, heaps of smashed brickwork half-buried in the mud, and other debris – past a tank which apparently had been blown to pieces from the interior – until we reached the railway line, close to which were the remains of several overturned trucks.

Here we branched to our left, and had proceeded about another 200 yards when suddenly there was a loud pop from the direction of the German lines and in a few seconds we heard the ominous whine of a German shell, which increased in sound to a roaring screech until, with a final rush, it dropped and exploded only about 20 yards from us. That was the first of hundreds as we soon discovered, for shells began to drop like leaves in autumn and we had to look round for the nearest cover. But to look for cover in that desolate wilderness was like looking for sugar in Army porridge. However, we spotted a few baulks of timber resting against some masonry and made a dive for those. At least, there was not much 'dive' about it. Handicapped as we were with mud up to our knees, it was more like the wallowing and splashing of disturbed ducks. Anyhow, we just got to our frail cover in time, for the enemy put up a barrage in the hopes of annihilating half the British Army (to judge by the intensity of the bombardment). This state of affairs lasted nearly four hours and the dawn found us still crouching in our cramped position, wedged between the timber and the crumbling masonry, half blinded by the flashes, choking with the fumes and smoke, and deafened by the explosions of the shells which continually dropped in close proximity to our precarious position.

However, at last, the tornado ceased and we were able to emerge once more, to continue our journey.

We eventually arrived at our destination which was a pillbox at the end of a duck board track and when we shouldered our gun, tripod, ammunition, etc. each of us had a burden which was more suitable for a camel than a human being! Our heavy loads and the conditions underfoot, combined with the fact that it was now daylight – which enabled the enemy to snipe at us at will – made it extremely difficult for us to get back to our pillbox, but we managed it eventually. On arriving, I reported to the officer and handed over the gun kit which we had so difficultly salved. By this time, my gun team (and myself) were so fatigued that we simply collapsed on the floor and as we had undergone such a trying experience to save the gun and ammunition, we were allowed to sleep the best way we could, until we were required for sentry duty again, which, by the way, was only a few hours.

Later on during that evening, Bert's team were pleasantly surprised to be relieved by two gun teams of the 215th Machine Gun Company. After another tedious journey through slush and over duck-boards, they eventually arrived at the nearest usable road to the line, and after a wait of five hours, a number of lorries arrived and took them back to huts near Vlamertinghe. There they were to remain until 10 November, when certain units were given orders for the front line once more. Bert was one of those left behind and valued such a reprieve.

The Third Battle of Ypres was effectively over. Passchendaele Ridge had been captured and the German Army had been forced to divert its resources to the Ypres Salient, allowing the French Army further south to recover from the earlier Nivelle Offensive. The 'bite and hold' system of smaller offensives that was designed to seize and retain ground appeared to have worked, albeit at a high cost in terms of the now seemingly unavoidable high casualty rates on both sides. For Bert Atkins, however, time away from the fighting would be filled by more personal concerns.

Spots appeared on my arms and I needed no telling to know that I had
scabies again due probably to the fact that I had been obliged to keep
my clothes on for weeks. So, on November 13th, I reported sick and
was marked for hospital. An ambulance took me to the Main Dressing
Station and thence I went by motor lorry to the hospital at Wormhout.
The treatment here for scabies was rough and very painful but it
appeared to be efficacious. Firstly an RAMC orderly shaved all surplus
hair from my body, arms and legs. Then I had to immerse myself in a
bath of almost scalding hot water, until I felt (and looked) like a boiled
lobster. The next stage was the most painful part of the operation
though. I was given a hard scrubbing all over from head to foot with
a very stiff brush, which actually felt like a wire brush! This treatment
of course left me bleeding and scratched all over. I understood the idea
was to open up the pores of the skin where scabies microbes might
be lurking, so that they could be dealt with by the next part of the
programme. This consisted of my being painted bright yellow all over
(except my face) with a mixture of sulphur and iodine. After a week
or so I was judged to be fit enough to return to duty in the trenches.

Bert Atkins (b.1898)

After leaving the army, Bert spent 42 years in the Civil Service,
mainly as a Post Office telecommunications engineer. He
contributed to the Second World War through service in the
Home Guard, ultimately donating his battledress to the Imperial
War Museum. Returning to his civilian engineering career, Bert
was heavily involved in planning the cabling system for the new
BBC Television Centre built at Wood Lane in London in 1960,
and retired to Pinner in Middlesex soon after completing this
major project. IWM's last correspondence with Bert was in
November 1979, when he had reached the age of 80.

10 | Gilbert

THE GERMAN SPRING OFFENSIVE MARCH 1918

In the thick mist, at 5am on the morning of March 21st, the storm broke

By the beginning of 1918, the war had become an integral part of peoples' everyday lives for those based on the home front or on active service overseas. With no immediate end in sight, it seemed as if the fighting would continue indefinitely. Yet the fifth year of the conflict would prove to be characterised by dramatic twists and turns, which led to great uncertainty over the future. Following the initial events of spring 1918, it seemed to many that the Allies may well be fighting a losing battle.

Recent progress by the Allies on the Western Front had been limited, despite the perceived success of the ground-breaking use of armoured tanks during the Battle of Cambrai in November 1917. Across France and Belgium, the stalemate between the two opposing armies remained very much in place. Greater momentum had been achieved by the fighting around Passchendaele in the Third Battle of Ypres, yet the enormous cost in lives would result in the battle being regarded as a sequel to 1916's disappointing Somme rather than a more obvious strategic victory.

Among those British troops maintaining the front line defences in France was Gilbert Laithwaite, born in Dublin in July 1894 and the eldest of four children. Attending the Jesuit boarding school at Clongowes in County Kildare, he had won a scholarship to Trinity College Oxford where he distinguished himself as a classical scholar. Commissioned as a 2nd Lieutenant with the Special Reserve, Gilbert found himself attached from April 1917 to the 10th Battalion Lancashire Fusiliers, part of 52nd Brigade of the 17th Division. In March 1918 he was based with the Battalion in the Havrincourt Salient, west of the town of Cambrai. Rumours of an imminent German offensive were widespread, but neither Gilbert nor his comrades quite appreciated how near at hand such an attack was.

We had been warned to expect it, first on the 2nd, then on the 5th, then on the 8th, but remained rather incredulous. On the evening of the 7th, as we sat in our cosy little dugout, Brigade Signals Twigg rang up to ask about our communications with our companies across the canal, and talked so indiscreetly and in so troubled a tone that I began to believe. After it I turned to the Colonel and said, 'Do you really expect an attack tomorrow, Sir? Twigg seems so worried'. He laughed and said, 'Oh well, you never know, you know'. I said, 'Well Sir, I'll risk it and undo my boots', which I did. Nothing happened of course, but all through this tour we were continually on edge.

Following the overthrow of the Tsar the previous year and the establishment of a new Bolshevik government, the Treaty of Brest-Litovsk signed with the German Empire on 3 March 1918 ended Russia's participation in the war. The main consequence of this peace was to free up a significant number of German troops who, previously engaged in maintaining the Eastern Front against the Russians, could be moved to the Western Front and thereby allow the implementation of a major offensive in those sectors. The United States had formally declared war against Germany in April 1917, and with troops of the American Expeditionary Force expected to arrive in significant numbers in France and Belgium in the spring of

1918 in order to bolster the Allied armies, the pressure was on for Germany to act quickly in order to seize the advantage.

Gilbert's 52nd Brigade moved up to relieve the 51st Brigade in the front line sector north-west of Flesquières on the evening of Monday 18 March.

The front was comparatively quiet at the moment. It was about 6.45: a beautifully clear March evening, a brilliant sun setting behind us through the high black leafless trees of Havrincourt Wood. There was no shelling, but the road packed with men and transport waiting till 7pm should come and the dusk allow them to cross the ridge west of Havrincourt Village and go forward. Looking behind, one could see more limbers winding down the plank road. To our front, over the ridge, were no less than five Boche balloons, and we could not understand why the enemy made no effort to shell the track and the slag heap, unless it was that the sun being in the eyes of his observers, they could not see the congestion along the road. The sector, all considered, was a good one. Our defences were extremely strong and every effort had been made to secure the front against any possibility of a breakthrough. In the first three months of 1918 the Fifth Corps were said to have put out as much wire as the whole Expeditionary Force had done in 1916.

Tuesday 19 March passed uneventfully, with the evening providing an unusual form of entertainment as Gilbert and others based in the Battalion Headquarters were able to observe gas being projected into the German lines west of the nearby canal. The following day brought the latest reports of a possible enemy offensive.

About 10pm a message came in from Brigade saying that the Fifth Army on our right had captured prisoners who declared that the attack was to come off next morning, March 21st, and ordering special precautions. We sent it out to companies and went to bed. Headquarters and

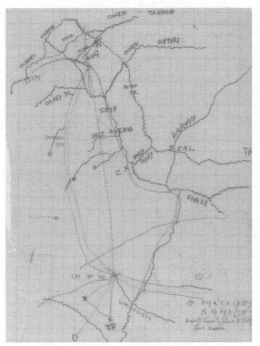

Sketch drawn by Gilbert Laithwaite, showing
the trench system where he was based when the
German Spring Offensive began on 21 March 1918

*Companies alike were by now so hardened to similar alarms, and so
sure that all possible precautions had been taken, that it was not taken
quite so seriously as it deserved. The night passed quietly.*

As Wednesday night disappeared with Thursday's dawn, it would
prove to be the last opportunity for calm that Gilbert would enjoy
for some considerable time.

*In a thick mist, at 5am on the morning of March 21st, the storm
broke. At 5.10am, as we lay asleep in our dugout in Whitehall
[trench], we were wakened by the servants calling Gas. Up in the
trench one heard a continuous hammering and ringing of gas gongs*

and bells, which for the moment reminded one of a London fire alarm. The gas curtains were all drawn on the steps, and the smell within the dugout very faint indeed. We blinked at one another, grinned uncomfortably, and thought that the Fifth Army prisoner had perhaps told the truth for once, and that the big show had arrived. We got on to the companies, who reported an intense gas barrage, with a good deal of intermixed shelling: all were standing to in respirators, and as yet there were no gas casualties. At the same time the line to Brigade went. We reported our situation by pigeon.

At 7.15 we breakfasted, talking over the situation. The companies reported a slackening in the gas, and an increase in the high explosive. While all tended to show that we were in the real attack, the situation was still too obscure to make it certain that it was not merely a raid on the grand scale, or an attempt to pinch the Flequières Salient.

I went up on top – the mist still hung, and the air was clogged with gas, I have never seen such a concentration. Overhead was a most extraordinary hissing sound – our shells whistling over without any semblance of a break, his guns replying vigorously: loud crashes from a 5.9 inch barrage falling on the Havrincourt-Moeuvres Road immediately in our rear. The noise was so great, and the whole thing so immense, that one's nerves steadied automatically. At 7.55am a message from A Company reported heavy shelling of the front line, and ten minutes later a runner from the West Yorks brought messages – timed 7.15 – from their company on our side of the canal reporting heavy trench mortars on the front line and several enemy aircraft over it. We felt that things could not be much longer delayed, and made arrangements for the destruction of all papers and the mustering of Headquarters as soon as word should come from the front.

Although its full scale remained unknown to Gilbert at this time, a major German offensive had indeed been launched on a vast extent across a wide front. Aimed at the British Fifth and Third Armies based on the Somme in front of St Quentin, the initial German goal was to break through the Allied lines and advance northwest towards the sea, pushing the British into retreat and separating them from the French further south.

Front and support systems were deluged with thousands of gas shells, mixed with high explosive: communication trenches and junctions barraged, all avenues of approach for reinforcing troops blocked by a chain of fire. Simultaneously, all rear Headquarters transport lines and heavy guns were subjected to a heavy bombardment from long-range high velocity guns. In the bank of the Canal du Nord the deep dugouts of 52nd Brigade Headquarters were blown in and their locality so thoroughly dealt with that no message by a Brigade Runner reached us in front all day. Within an hour from the opening of the barrage, the units holding the forward area were isolated from their brigades: by 6am there was no longer any communication backward – cable trenches were blown in, air lines cut, ordinary cross country wires smashed as soon as mended, while the mist rendered visual signalling impossible and pigeons uncertain.

This sudden lack of reliable communication resulted in considerable confusion among the various units in the front line. Forward battalions such as Gilbert's were unsure of the actual position and extent of the German attack, and so were forced to make unilateral decisions and follow actions which seemed the most sensible given the limited information at their disposal. In effect, they had to fight their own battle.

Young staggered in from C Company, bringing a report of the situation as it had been when he left the line an hour before – it was bad. By 8.20am the front line had been flattened and its garrison buried: the communication trenches were blown in, parts of the support system razed. He reported that as yet there was no sign of enemy attack. As he finished, a further message from the observation post reported that the barrage had shifted from the front line on to the support system and rear trenches. It was hastily decided to concentrate on the defence of the Carey [trench] line in the event of the front line going, and a message to this effect was made out for the brigade. I wrote it down for the CO and had just signed it when a last message came through – 'Enemy coming over on our right'. It was 10.25am. We all jumped up, shook hands and wished good luck.

All Headquarters were got out on top except two signallers, a servant and the orderly room clerk who was destroying all papers. Maps, diaries, letters, all went with them. On top the mist had cleared, the gas was disappearing in the morning sun – George Street to our right was being heavily shelled, and 5.9's were falling just over Headquarters on the road behind. We all got rifles and bandoliers, and at this point got some heart from the sight of the Regimental Sergeant Major, Newman, who, flat on his back in the trench, was popping up SOS rockets with intense and deliberate satisfaction. Hardly had we got lined along the trench than a vicious enfilade machine gun fire made us duck our heads. Out to the north, in the area of the 51st Division in front of Demicourt and Louverval, we could see a crushing barrage landing some distance along the front as far to the north as we could see. Looking through field glasses we saw our people reinforcing there in artillery formation, across the open, and the shells bursting among the groups.

But our own situation seemed too serious to allow much gazing round – we saw little hope of finishing the morning. Pegrum [the second in command] had now come back: he reported the front line flat, and its defenders buried, saying 'You could walk on tin hats all along it', but was otherwise reassuring as to the effect of the fire. He had seen all company commanders, arranged that Carey should be the ultimate line beyond which there must be no retreat, and had fixed up the question of reinforcement by the support companies. He reported about sixty casualties in A and D Companies. To our front was a rise in the ground,

along which ran Lock Trench, which completely shut off our view of
the actual forward area. We watched this crest with eager eyes, every
moment expecting to see the remnants of our own people come over it
or, worse still, the Boche. As we watched, we saw file into it a line of tin
hats – our glasses showed that they were ours: they lined the crest, which
saved them from the machine gun bullets, and waited quietly.

The limited communication and general confusion caused by the
intense shelling meant that the only definite facts known to Gilbert
were that their sector's front line had been shelled to bits, leaving
them to fall back on the Carey trench line for defence.

For fully half an hour we stood lined along Whitehall, rifles ready,
our eyes glued to the line of tin hats on the ridge to our front, waiting
eagerly for the seeming inevitable to happen, and yet nothing changed.
At last the Colonel said, 'I can't stand this any longer. I must go
forward and find out the situation' and strode off through the machine
gun bullets, over the top. As one stood and waited, one thought with
curious detachment of how people at home were just now going about
their business, not yet knowing that anything was happening out of
the ordinary, and thinking of the many hundreds of us who would be
done with before anyone at home suspected what was taking place.
But it was only for a moment – one could not dwell on anything
except the situation all around.

At this moment Lance Corporal Davies arrived back from Brigade
HQ and gave an astonishing account of the effects upon it of the
German barrage.

Brigade were, he said, literally imprisoned in their dugouts in the canal
bank, and so thoroughly that a wretched Staff Officer who in the
early morning had gone to General Office in pyjamas was still stuck
there, while the Brigade runner staff were unwilling to let anyone go

forward to the front line, regarding it as certain and useless death. We were pleased to hear of the aesthete in pyjamas, and more pleased to hear that Brigade was getting its share of the war, but this was nothing to our satisfaction when on opening the letters which Davies had brought up, the first turned out to be a chit from the Staff Captain asking whether we wished to use the vacancies allotted to us for a course at Auxi-le-Chateau on March 26th!

Meanwhile, the Colonel returned from his excursion to what could now be considered the new British front line, and brought good news.

We had stemmed the attack, though we had lost most of our front line and had been driven back to the support system. It was difficult to realise for the moment that on our front at any rate the attack had failed: our first duty was to inform Brigade, and after a lengthy and profane telephone conversation with the observation post, who still had some pigeons, we persuaded them to send back a situation report for us. The Colonel on his return said, 'The brutes shot the Trench Mortar officer as he came up the steps of his dugout, after he had put up his hands'. This spread like wildfire, but we found afterwards that it was not correct. When the Boche suddenly arrived at the dugout entrance and shouted down 'surrender', he had doubled upstairs firing his revolver at them, and so was very naturally shot down.

The fog had now dispersed and the sun shone out brilliantly – a typical March morning, clear and cold. Gilbert and his fellow officers enjoyed a lunch of Irish stew, tinned peaches and whiskey while taking advantage of the relative quiet to discuss the morning's occurrences.

The West Yorks sent in to say that they too had lost their front line and that they would cooperate with us in our proposed counter attack. At 3pm orders came from Brigade by a returning runner that the counter attack was to be cancelled for the present and further orders awaited. At 3.15pm an urgent message came in from the Manchesters on our right, reporting 1,000 Boche moving west towards Hughes Trench, and we immediately warned the companies and prepared to stand to again. But this menace was disposed of for us by D Company and their Lewis guns, which opened fire on the Boche as they deployed and decimated them, the attack collapsing in disorder.

Shelling continued heavily and indiscriminately all afternoon, and the reply of our batteries grew feebler: we were harassed by numerous red-bodied aeroplanes which hovered over Headquarters and came low enough to see everything that happened. Now that no reinforcements had been sent up, and that our counter attack had been cancelled, we felt a little grimly that it must have been decided we should hold the forward area at any cost, and give time for the guns to get to their new positions and for fresh divisions to arrive. We did not realise the extent of the attack, or that it would be some days yet before it was definitely decided where to stem it. Nor did we realise that our comparative peace that afternoon was due to nothing more than the fact that our flanks had been driven in to the north and south. We knew nothing of the position save what we could see.

We sat in our open-air mess about tea time, when a plane swooped suddenly right down over us, and got away again despite vigorous firing, aided by much profanity expended by Howarth on the luckless gunner from the Lewis gun post just outside. Five minutes later we were enfiladed with 4.2's which hissed down with a rush just over our heads and burst with a crash twenty yards further down the trench. The noise was abominable: they missed us by too narrow a margin to be comfortable, and we fled downstairs till things grew quieter and had some tea.

By 6pm it was decided that Gilbert would make an excursion forward to the Battalion's front line companies. Accompanied by Ready, one of the signallers, and carrying a supply of SOS rockets, they climbed out of the trench at HQ and went over the top towards Lock trench in the gathering twilight.

The ground was greatly cut up by the morning's shelling, but things were comparatively quiet. Everyone was very keen for any news of the general position – all we could tell them was that Corps HQ was reported to have been heavily shelled that morning. This caused laughter, the idea of respectable Brigadiers or Corps Commanders under fire proving too much. I went down the trench to Ship, the main communication trench – thence forward along what seemed an interminable and unrecognisable way. The trench was much knocked about, though in no place absolutely blown in. As one drew nearer Carey it became very bad – in fact almost level. At the point where Carey joined Ship, the whole place was so battered that for a moment I could not tell which way to go. It was getting dark – machine gun bullets were whizzing over aimlessly, and there was a good deal of desultory shelling all about the forward area. Leaping over the ruins of Carey, I soon got into a fairly decent part where the majority of A Company were. The men were fagged, but very good tempered. Barrow promised to try to push on and said that the men were keen enough but had had a very trying time – rations had very largely perished in the bombardment, while fires were of course impossible.

He told me how that morning, just before the Boche came over, he had found in Ship Trench a man carrying a ration bag. He stopped him and said, 'What are you doing here? Where is your rifle? Why aren't you in the front line?' The man said plaintively, 'Please sir, I'm the postman and these are the Company letters: I can't get round to deliver them'. Barrow guffawed when he thought of this faithful servant, burdened with letters, whose owners were no longer, for the most part, able to read them.

As we struggled on, an excited group rushed up – they had that moment escaped from A Company's dugout and through the Boche lines. The dugout, they said, had not yet been entered by the Boche though there were Boche sentries over both entrances. When the Boche arrived in the morning he threw down stick bombs, but had not the courage to follow them up: the first bomb burst just outside the signal office at the foot of the stairs, wounded Overton in the leg and caught Gordon in the back of the head – he became unconscious and lay there all day, moaning and wailing till he died about 6pm, a good and pleasant man whom I much liked, and a sad loss. Whittam said, to my sorrow, 'The Powerbuzzer and the Fuller phone are both quite safe, sir: we took great care of them!' I had hoped against hope that Gordon might have destroyed them, as no doubt he would have had he lived, and suggested to Barrow a patrol which might release any others who might be in the dugout and possibly retrieve the Powerbuzzer as well.

The 'power buzzer' was a very basic communications system designed to send a signal via ground induction; a metal spike was driven into the ground and signals passed through it using Morse and other simple codes. The Fullerphone was a rather more sophisticated telephone system which relied on wires. Both pieces of equipment were essential for communication purposes and to have discarded them, making them available for the Germans to requisition for their own use, was a serious matter.

Whittam told us that the Boche sentries at his end had gone off for the moment, leaving their packs and equipment dumped. Barrow agreed as to a patrol, and we made up a patrol of six from among the men. We went to the bombstep and climbed over – I was third. In the trench on the other side was a long black bar. Barrow said, 'Take great care of this – it's a trap – pass it back that none is to walk on it or touch it'. We did not, but passed on and almost immediately found dumped on the side a new and complete Granatenwerfer [A grenade-throwing trench mortar used by German infantry] with wooden stand, full tool bag and two bags of bombs – it had never been used. Going on further, we passed ten or a dozen dumped Boche packs, rifles, tin hats, etc. Looking eagerly at each one as we passed, I got a full identification – soldier's book, diary, paybook and letters – they were the 242nd Saxon Regiment. There were no bodies. We pushed on, not without misgivings, as the right wall of the trench was well blown in and had numerous gaps, which caused us qualms about being taken in rear, till we got to the junction of Sun and Ship. As we reached the old Trench Mortar dugout I suddenly saw a number of tall figures rush out wearing Boche tin hats lapped in sacking. They threw bombs at us, luckily unsuccessfully, and Winstanley on our side got in both with bomb and with bayonet. But it was clear that it was no good going on, as the enemy was on the lookout, and we withdrew gradually, and unpursued, down the trench. As we did so a Verey light floated down and settled over the trench right beside us, while we crouched waiting for it to fall. It fell, and spat itself out deliberately and slowly, while machine guns were set going overhead from both flanks. But the Boche did not follow up, and we got back safely with our identification and the Granatenwerfer, which I carried off as spoil to Headquarters. With difficulty, because of the damage to the trenches, we got back to HQ where I dined greedily, wrote an intelligence report for Brigade, and went to bed weary about 11.30pm.

Gilbert slept for only a couple of hours before news arrived suggesting that orders were about to be received to withdraw back further to the Havrincourt Ridge. Around 2.30am this intention was confirmed, with the Battalion instructed to evacuate the forward system as quietly as possible. A protecting patrol was sent out to engage the Germans while this was happening.

Torrens, after issuing the orders and making arrangements, said, 'I can just imagine the Boche Brigadier who is at the moment probably camouflaging a report on the day's operations, and talking of the strength of the enemy's position: he'll call the runner back, and amend to read "By a fresh attack, at 3am we drove in the enemy outposts and forced him to evacuate the salient!"' We warned the observation post, about which someone luckily remembered; the companies got safely away, Headquarters moved off last. The whole move was carried out without the Boche knowing anything about it. Before leaving we set fire to our Headquarters dugout. Chairs, tables, the Granatenwerfer and its stock of bombs (I kept the spirit level) – all went in. Ashworth led off Headquarters, all officers carrying bags of rations or water tins (mine were onions) and everyone with a load. I found myself in rear with the Regimental Sergeant Major, an old Regular soldier. He said, 'I suppose, Sir, another Division is coming up tonight to take over the line from us?' I said, 'I'm afraid we're the last British troops who'll look on this district for some time to come'. It was rather typical – none of the men could for a moment understand why we were clearing out, especially after our successful morning.

It must have taken nearly an hour to get from Whitehall to the crest of the hill, and loud and deep were the curses on the unhappy Ashworth, who was leading the way. It was pitch black, bitterly cold, and the trench winding steeply up the slope, little better than a drain. In front of me, struggling knee deep through the clinging slimy mud was Theobald the sniper, burdened with two water tins in addition to his kit: he was in a bad way and kept falling behind – we were all too heavily laden ourselves to be able to help him. The RSM and I tried to keep him going; once he quite gave way and said, 'I can't do it, Sir: I can't do it. I'm crucified with these tins and this equipment'. It was a relief after we got to the top of the hill, and the sunken road above Railway Trench, blocked with the trunks of fallen trees and curiously quiet except for the subdued talk of the men and casual movement up and down. The old front line was very still – no shelling, now and then a rifle shot, an occasional Verey light: only to our left gas shells kept rushing over with slow persistency and bursting with an oily flop in Havrincourt.

Arrived at their new defensive position, Gilbert reported to the Colonel who instructed him to go forward to prepare their new Battalion Headquarters.

Outside the dawn was breaking, but a thick mist hung over everything – it was about 5am, cold and raw. I picked up some of the men of headquarters and walked down the road to reconnoitre our new home. It was a depressing contrast to the luxurious and well-ordered headquarters we had evacuated the night before – a derelict trench, overgrown with weeds, almost untrodden since December 1917 – at its farther end a small dump of dud anti-aircraft shells and Boche potato-masher bombs. There were three dugouts – all old Boche, and so with their entrances now facing him. The next thing was to get communication established: we had of course no wire, but had saved all our instruments. I took Keough the signaller, and we went together across the open through the mist to salvage wire in Havrincourt village.

While we were getting a signal line going to the Companies, Smith had been wandering round. He now came up and said, 'Come along to the road – I've a sight to show you – two dead men'. I jeered at him as a ghoul, but went, for some morbid reason. The road was a bad sight: a barrage of 5.9 had clearly been dropped right along it, and there were shell holes every couple of feet. We got to the crossroads and saw a horrid sight – Smith's two dead men. Both were from the Royal Naval Division and wore the little anchor divisional sign. Both were quite dead and had been for hours: they were transport drivers in the RFA. One lay flat on his back in the middle of the road, face upwards, hands outstretched, apparently unwounded, his breast pocket unbuttoned and the paybook showing out through it, a look of entire peace and rest on his bloodless, waxy face – it struck one by its complete detachment and quiet. The other man was kneeling in the middle of the road, one arm covered in blood-stained bandages, head forward, body in a crouching attitude, his face contorted, in his back the wound which had killed him: this road crossing must have been used the evening before as a temporary dressing station, and one could imagine how he had crouched down to avoid the shell he heard coming, but had had no shelter and no escape. We left them, a grisly pair, and went back to our trench.

Despite death being a common occurrence in trench warfare, the sight of dead soldiers could clearly still affect a seasoned soldier at unexpected moments.

Harrison and I made our way across the road and towards the canal in search of the Companies stationed in the other half of City. The mist was lifting a little. We could see a couple of hundred yards; we remembered how greatly a similar mist had helped the Boche twenty-four hours earlier, and thought rather gratefully that for once the weather was helping us. There was practically no shelling as yet and we pushed on overland as quickly as we could, when suddenly a 4.2 bursting just in front of us with the most horrid and unexpected suddenness made us rush to the cover of the trench. The chief impression made on me by the visit was of the complete change in our circumstances. Thirty six hours before we had been well fed, fresh, comfortably housed, looking forward to relief: now we held a bare trench line, shallow, and devoid of any cover; our rations were limited; our fires reduced to one or two; men and officers alike unshaven and tired after twenty-four hours fighting and retreating – the future obscure and threatening. It was true that everyone was cheerful, good tempered, and anxious to be of use, but it was noticeable that the uncertainty of the situation told markedly more on officers than on the men, and that while the men were prepared to take things as they came with their usual lightheartedness, the officers welcomed any opportunity to talk things over and relieve their minds by frank discussion of possibilities. We left the Companies in good fettle and made our way back to Headquarters.

There, Gilbert was presented with detailed orders for the retreat of the three brigades of the 17th Division several miles further west, as far as the town of Ytres. All routes had been arranged with collecting posts, transport lines and dressing stations. Gilbert still lacked reliable information about the bigger situation regarding the German offensive, and so these new orders to retreat were received with some surprise. At the moment the plan of retreat was only provisional, with definite movement orders arriving later that evening on Friday 22 March. More immediately, however, at 3.00pm that afternoon a crushing barrage fell on their whole front from Hermies to Havrincourt, and with particular ferocity below the crest of the Havrincourt Ridge around the new Battalion Headquarters dugout.

The barrage lasted in full violence till 3.30pm, the dugout shaking under it while pieces of mortar and chalk pattered down the steps, candles went out under the crump of 5.9's landing overhead and were relighted, and we looked at one another and waited for the entrance to be blown in. A message from the front reported the enemy in Colin Street, in full pack, climbing out of the trench. Finally a pigeon message was made out giving our situation, and I took the pigeon up to the trench to set it off. Just as I did so, the barrage lifted from us and shifted on to the Valley and Yorkshire Spoil Heap behind us, particular attention being paid to the road crossing and all avenues for reinforcement. It was a splendid sight, a line of earth spouts all along – as I looked down I thought of the orders for withdrawal we had seen and wondered what chance we should have of getting away through the bottleneck, deciding finally that open order down the slope, across the Grand Ravine, and trust in God was the only answer. I sent up the unlucky pigeon, which had already been in the line more than the prescribed 48 hours: it rose high over the ridge, circled in a dazed way through the shell bursts and the rattle-rattle of machine guns for a few seconds, then, to my horror, flew off straight as a die towards the Boche lines. Luckily the message gave away no secrets, but I did not venture to tell the CO, nor was I, fortunately, questioned.

We had a brief lull, during which I wandered up and down outside the headquarters trench: gunfire continued heavy, but was not particularly directed at us. About 5pm a further heavy attack developed against Havrincourt and Hermies. We were lucky; the sunken road to our left was heavily shelled, and Havrincourt to our right shrouded in a mass of thick black smoke as shell after shell burst in the ruined houses at the edge of the village. The contrast was complete: along the ridge the rolling fumes of smoke, the crash of the bursting shells, the vivid colours of the rockets, the pink clouds where a burst took place in red brick ruins, the trench lined with tin-hatted men rifle in hand, and the continuous and unintermitting rat-tat of machine guns from beyond the ridge – the clear and peaceful twilight of a late March evening, the red glow of the setting sun over Hermies, the quiet sky, the quiet wood behind.

In those two or three hours SOS went up more than a dozen times from our front, till finally we grew hardened to it – there was nothing to be done save see it through, and no help to be given or obtained. I went up and down the trench several times to see how people were. During one of our stand-to's, a wounded boy looking for the Advanced Dressing Station came along the trench, his chest all blood, and Harrison, my servant, courageously took him through the heavy shelling on the Hermies/Havrincourt Road and to the ADS in the Quarry, reporting on return that this had had a direct hit earlier in the day.

By 8.oopm that evening, things had quietened down. It was dark by now, and Gilbert could witness a column of smoke rising across the ridge, lightened by occasional bursts of flame, from the direction of his old dugout in Whitehall trench which had been set on fire the night before. After dinner, he went on top and walked up and down for a while in the cool. The sky was light, though the moon was not yet fully up, the weather cold and frosty, and he was glad to return to the warmth of the brazier in his dugout.

Tired out, I went to sleep on the table. When I woke up, about 1.15, the orders had arrived: we were to evacuate the ridge, leaving covering parties, and to retire to the line of the Grand Ravine. Tommy Howarth was anxious to set fire to our dugout, but it was finally decided that by doing so we might betray our retreat to the Boche before he himself would have discovered it, and it was better to leave it. It was 2.30am on the morning of the 23rd March. Everything was now ready. We all gathered in the trench on top – there was a brilliant moon; everything quiet save for an occasional Verey light; the night very cold. The Colonel gave the word and we moved off, thinking a little bitterly that with the ridge we now evacuated went the last of our gains in the Cambrai offensive, and wondering how much further it might prove necessary to continue our retreat. We felt no little anxiety throughout – first lest the enemy should discover what was happening and strike in the middle of our relief; next lest we should be shelled while passing down the road by the side of the Yorkshire Spoil Heap, which would have been a death trap without escape.

We got thankfully out of the shadow of the slagheap into the moonlight at the bottom of the hill and found a scene of great activity – light burning at the entrance to a dugout, ration boxes being carried off and allotted, numbers of men moving to and fro. At the crossroads we saw Lindley, the Brigade Major, and made for him, full of questions about our kits, the general situation, the prospect of relief and how we had done. He was as bright and bustling as usual, and in the best of temper, declared to our amazement that we were the only Division which had held its own on an eighty mile front, that he thought we might be relieved in a day or two if the situation improved, but that the only available relief, the 19th Division, was fighting towards Doignies and beyond Velu. He hinted of special congratulations to the Brigade, and said that future moves remained uncertain, but that the 51st Brigade were to evacuate Hermies, in front of which there were 3,000 dead Boche, the sunken road being clogged with their bodies, and that the railway bridge over the Canal du Nord would be blown up at 4am – in about an hour's time. He cheered us all up immensely, and it was especially satisfactory to know that we were in the big show and that we had had such good luck.

Good luck indeed. Malcolm Brown, in *The Imperial War Museum Book of 1918: Year of Victory*, records that the German attack launched on 21 March resulted in 38,500 British casualties that day alone, while the Germans suffered nearer 40,000. While two thirds of the German casualties suffered wounds and in many cases would return to the fight, 28,000 of the British casualties were effectively lost to the battle: 7,000 dead, with an enormous 21,000 entering captivity as prisoners of war.

The offensive had resulted in the deepest advance by either side since the beginning of the war, yet exhaustion coupled with a failure to adequately supply its troops meant that the initial German successes were not followed up. The spring offensive had been designed as a monumental effort to crush the Allies and its immediate effect had been dramatic, yet the lack of a coherent German strategy and the British tactic of concentrating on defending key areas while giving up other ground of less value meant that the battle had failed to be as decisive as had been intended.

Subsequent attempts were made by the Germans to continue the attack – most notably on 9 April at the Battle of the Lys and on 27 May during the Third Battle of the Aisne – but the Second Battle of the Marne in July saw a final end to the offensive when French and American troops, including tanks, counter-attacked to prevent any further German advances. The tide would now turn in the Allies' favour, so that by the autumn of 1918 the situation on the Western Front would appear very different indeed from how the year had begun.

Gilbert Laithwaite (1894–1986)

After the Armistice, Gilbert joined the India Office where his important work included extending the vote among a large portion of the Indian population. From 1936 he served as principal private secretary to the Viceroy of India, before returning to Britain in 1943 as Assistant Under-Secretary of State for India. Having been knighted in 1941, in 1950 Sir Gilbert was appointed as the United Kingdom's first Ambassador to the Republic of Ireland, and the following year became High Commissioner to Pakistan. He served as Permanent Under-Secretary of State for Commonwealth Relations between 1955 and 1959. Following his retirement, Sir Gilbert played an active part in the life of the City of London as a director of various insurance companies. He died in 1986, aged 92.

I I | Arthur

ARMISTICE
NOVEMBER 1918

And after this, what is to become of us now?

The German offensive of spring 1918 had finally broken the deadlock of trench warfare and shown that it was possible for one side to make significant advances. As the German advance petered out due to exhaustion and over-confidence, it became the turn of the Allies to turn the tide of the fighting and begin the slow push eastwards, forcing the German Army back. The so-called 'Hundred Days Offensive' was characterised by a series of Allied attacks, beginning in August, which saw successes at Amiens and Albert before the Battles of the Hindenburg Line in September and October resulted in the strongly defended German positions being broken with surprising speed.

By this time, German troops were suffering from lack of food, inadequate weaponry and equipment and, perhaps worst of all, low morale. In contrast, the Allies had attacked in a unified manner and maintained a measured advance, taking full advantage of technology under the auspices of the 'All Arms Battle'. By employing more sophisticated artillery bombardment techniques including gas shells, adopting ground-strafing aircraft and armoured tanks and more heavily armed infantry troops, they were able to move towards ultimate victory. Successes elsewhere helped to drive the Allies forwards. The Palestine campaign had resulted in the victorious capture of Damascus on 1 October; Bulgaria had signed an armistice to bring an end to the campaign in Macedonia a few days before; and the final offensive against the Austrians on the River Piave at the end of October marked the end of the Italian campaign. It was on the Western Front, however, that the war had begun and, ultimately, would end.

Private Arthur Wrench, a soldier from Glasgow in his early 20s, had been serving with the 4th Battalion Seaforth Highlanders in France and Belgium since November 1915; his duties as a brigade runner involved the carrying of messages between officers and units, often throughout the most dangerous sectors of the front line. The summer of 1918 had seen his 51st Highland Division based around the Marne and Aisne, the same ground upon which the decisive battles had taken place at the very beginning of the war. As the autumn approached Arthur found himself moving eastwards in tandem with the Allied advance, which was met by strings of German prisoners being escorted in the opposite direction into captivity. From his location near Cambrai at the end of October 1918, the signs of an impending end to the conflict were becoming much more noticeable.

The morale of the German army must be very much shaken now and prisoners, too, declare that it is finished with them and Germany cannot win. That seems obvious to us also now and that alone, I am sure, is what actually keeps us going, for the strain on every one of us is tremendous. I am ready to drop right now.

By Monday 4 November the news was even more positive.

Tonight there is great news of further progress up the line. We don't even hear the guns now so that's something. And prisoners are being reckoned by the thousands instead of hundreds, so it's very gratifying to think that our side is still winning and so far there's been no further orders to move up again.

The beginning of November 1918 brought regular days of rain to northern France, and Arthur recorded how it poured through every hole and corner of his Cambrai billet. But the damp, miserable conditions could not prevent him and his comrades from feeling elation at the latest bit of good news on Tuesday 5 November.

There is an official report today that Austria has thrown up the sponge unconditionally and it has almost electrified us. So soon it will be Germany's turn to do likewise. The 22nd Corps HQ shifted to Valenciennes today too and to think that a <u>Corps</u> headquarters should make such a shift all at once to what was enemy ground the other day, a distance of 15 miles or so, is absolutely unprecedented. We've been talking about it ever since. It appears therefore that we are to be settled here for some time and there is every indication now that that unbelievable rumour, that the 51st Division may not be in action again, may be fully realised after all.

The respite in the fighting and the general feeling that the war was slowing down in preparation for a final ceasefire led many soldiers to reflect on their individual involvement, their personal fate and that of their family and friends. 8 November was a date with particular poignancy for Arthur as it marked the anniversary of his brother's death.

I'm just thinking that it's a year ago today since Bill was killed. Time does fly after all, though generally the minutes seem like hours and the hours like days. Yet I can hardly believe that it is so long since I came out here myself. And with it all, I am still to the fore with every prospect of surviving to the end at last and possessing that which fully justifies my hopes for a happier and brighter future. And to

*think that poor Bill paid the penalty of patriotism so soon! I wonder
what thanks he'll get for it, and we who survive too? Another year
has gone by since then. It has been a long year in many ways and I
wonder how the one to follow will go. If it is my lot yet to follow
Bill, there's no power on earth can say otherwise nor stop it but these
years of misery so far will then be all for nothing. It would still be
better if I had 'gone west' then, the same as Bill did. But I am still
alive though, somehow or other, and darned lucky at that, I suppose,
so long may I keep it up.*

Saturday 9 November saw Arthur visiting the small town of Iwuy,
a couple of miles north-east of Cambrai, where he met with some
old acquaintances including a school friend whom he had not seen
for many years. They enjoyed a cinema show before he mounted his
bicycle and started pedalling back towards his billets in the Saint-
Roch district of Cambrai.

*It was pitch dark and the road is still in an awful condition with shell
holes merely being filled up so that I had about the bumpiest and
sorest cycle runs in my whole life. A lot more civilians have returned
to their homes there too and the place is a lot better looking than it
was. On my return now I hear tonight that Mons has fallen. Mons!
Well, and that is just about where the war started too. Funny if it
should end there again after all.*

The following day brought confirmation that Mons had indeed
been recaptured by the Canadian Corps, who had also advanced for
miles beyond. The town had been the site for the first proper battle
of the war in August 1914 and had been under German occupation
for over four years.

*It is simply great news. I don't know how to say what I feel like
saying. It is quite impossible. Probably long after this is over I will*

be better able to express all these emotions that possess every one of us, for meantime I think we are all mad. It is officially announced that an armistice has been signed to take effect at eleven o'clock tomorrow, when hostilities will cease. Firing has ceased already on a certain part of the front to allow the German plenipotentiaries to come through the lines. And so what a racket. The Argylls band are out in force and even here we can hear them play. These drums are being beat as they never were beat before. I never dreamed the skins could stand such walloping, nor the pipes to sound so wild and grand. What a great and glorious feeling it is. The war is over and we have won. Out in the yard there is a crazy bonfire of boxes of German rockets and star shells and they are spurting and fizzling dangerously in every direction and, just like us, 'bursting' with enthusiasm at the glorious news. And the noise is almost deafening.

The momentous day finally arrived: an armistice would come into effect at 11.00am on Monday, 11 November 1918.

I think it is quite hopeless to try to describe what today means to us all. Meanwhile we are more subdued than we were and probably we are all pondering over the war that is past and the fact that we are among the survivors. It is almost unbelievable. The actual, official news of the armistice was issued at 8 o'clock this morning. It read, 'Hostilities cease at 11.00 hours. Today will be observed as a holiday'.

It was a holiday for everybody but Arthur, who had the important duty to deliver the news of the imminent armistice to certain units and officers in and around Cambrai. Wandering in the town through narrow streets and wider boulevards, Arthur was unfamiliar with the districts on the other side of the town from Saint Roch and found himself frequently lost, yet the good news he bore kept his mood buoyant.

I never had greater happiness in delivering despatches at any time before, lost or not. Now and then I overtook some civilians making their way along the streets and shouted the glad tidings to them. It was a study to observe the expressions on their faces, although for a brief moment some of them seemed to doubt me. Then I dismounted and told them over again that the war is finished and when they at last came to realise it was so and that I was telling the truth and the war was really to end at eleven o'clock, they would start and shout out of pure joy and I had a hard time taking myself away then to escape their embraces. Moreover, no unit ever received more welcome news nor received me either so gladly.

The feeling is general, and I cannot possibly describe it. One old man in Cambrai seemed to be scared out of his wits when I brushed past him and gave him the news. He too didn't understand me and started to bawl me out, perhaps for my carelessness in nearly running into him. So I got off and told him the story again and when he came to his senses he was most apologetic, then commenced shouting it out to this one and that whom he called by name and as if by magic a crowd gathered round to hear the news over again. It was fun. It almost seemed to stupefy them and it is just as hard for us to realise also that the war is over.

Eleven o'clock passed.

It was a somewhat solemn moment after the wild orgy last night to celebrate the passing of these years of so much bloodshed and cruelty and hardship. It seemed as if we had passed beyond the limits of this human existence altogether and into another barbaric realm: that we might have been asleep and dreaming horrible dreams all this while. Often I have thought that we would all wake up some day and find ourselves in our own beds as usual; that all our acquaintances at the front would turn out to be merely strangers and imaginary, dream companions; in fact, that the war never really existed at all and everything will be as normal as it was before. But meanwhile we seem to be in a state of semi-consciousness; an irresponsible, nervous condition like being aroused in the morning and only half awake. It is all so mysterious to have lived through so much danger, seen so much death and often wished for it myself too, and yet clung desperately to the very thread of life itself.

An hour ago it was war and now it is peace, yet the transition is too subtle for us to comprehend at the moment since we are not actually in action. I wonder what it was like in the front line? And if they kept on firing up to the very last minute, or if there was any shooting after that? Well, I should not worry now. I have come through it after all and I pray and hope to God there will be no more of such political misunderstanding and madness that will start off another war. Surely this is the last war that will ever be between any civilised nations. And after this, what is to become of us now? Are we to be better off or worse and shall we say to Germany, 'Let us forget and forever henceforth be at peace?'

Tonight now the cheers and tumult have once more turned into a riot of wild enthusiasm. It is pandemonium and I am sure we must all be mad. From one extreme to another. Even as I used to think that someday we would 'wake up' and find the war was over, so now I hope we will all sober up and come back to our senses. The bonfire is blazing again out in the courtyard and boxes of German star shells and signal flares are being piled on to feed it. They are bursting and flying all over the shop, as if they too were revelling in a new found freedom. It is certainly dangerous and someone is liable to get hurt. Even last night we were still exposed to the possibility of an air raid yet none of us gave it a thought. But not tonight, and it is a unique way of enjoying the fireworks that were originally made for another purpose.

Yet this is all very superficial and while we are letting ourselves get loose it is certain that each one of us has time to give a thought of regret for our late pals who have 'gone west' and have not been spared to become mad with us as well. So it is yet to be seen whether the price they have paid will be in vain or will be truly honoured and appreciated. And we who will return to tell people what war really is surely hope that 11am this day will be of great significance to generations to come.

Arthur Wrench (1895–1990)

Writing to the Imperial War Museum in 1985, at the age of 90, Arthur explained that 'On my leave from the Front I left my notes at home, then after demobilisation I wrote them up in this diary so as to be intelligible and understood but with no change whatever … I am surely blessed that I survived the war with one small wound'. By then he was living with his wife Peggy in New York City, having moved to the United States of America some years before. In one of the last letters written to the museum, Arthur declared himself to be 'honoured that my war diary will find a permanent place in your Imperial War Museum'. He died in 1990, at the age of 94.

Sources

Rosie *Edinburgh Evening News,*
31 October 1905; author's private
correspondence with Kitty Brewster's
descendants, Kit Hesketh-Harvey
and Margaret Woodley; IWM,
Private Papers of Miss R A Neal
(Documents.1441), manuscript
account undated but written circa
October 1914.

Hugh IWM, Private Papers of Captain
H C L Heywood (Documents.801),
manuscript extracts from
contemporary letters.

Eric IWM, Private Papers of Colonel Sir
Eric Gore-Browne (Documents.256),
typescript extracts from contemporary
letters; Nick Lloyd, *Loos 1915*
(Tempus Publishing, 2006).

Herbert IWM, Private Papers of Captain
H Ward (Documents.22831), manuscript
diary and expanded typescript memoir
written circa 1973; Trevor Henshaw,
The Sky Their Battlefield II (Fetubi
Books, 2014).

Fred IWM, Private Papers of F J Murfin
(Documents.14), typescript memoir
written in 1965; *Brigadier General Sir
James Edmonds, Official History of the
Great War: Military Operations France
and Belgium 1916, vol I* (1932, IWM
reprint); David Boulton, *Objection
Overruled* (MacGibbon & Kee, 1967);
John Rae, *Conscience and Politics: The
British Government and the Conscientious
Objector to Military Service 1916–19*
(Oxford University Press, 1970).

Kit IWM, Private Papers of Vice
Admiral C Caslon (Documents.10850),
typescript memoir written in 1923;
Peter Hart, *The Somme* (Weidenfeld &
Nicolson, 2005).

Lawrence IWM, Private Papers of
Captain L Gameson (Documents.612),
typescript memoir first drafted in 1923;
Peter Hart, *The Somme.*

Bobby IWM, Private Papers of Miss
G M West (Documents.7142),
manuscript diary.

Bert IWM, Private Papers of A L
Atkins (Documents.10767), typescript
memoir written in 1978 but based on
contemporary diary notes.

Gilbert IWM, Private Papers
of Sir Gilbert Laithwaite
(Documents.12262), typescript
memoir, undated but written soon after
the events described; Malcolm Brown,
*The Imperial War Museum Book of
1918: Year of Victory* (Sidgwick &
Jackson, 1999).

Arthur IWM, Private Papers of A E Wrench
(Documents.3834), typescript diary.

Credits

Rosie Private Papers of Miss
R A Neal (Documents.1441) ©The
Estate of Miss R A Neal; Photograph
©Photographer's Estate

Hugh Private Papers of Captain
H C L Heywood (Documents.801)
©The Estate of Captain H C L
Heywood

Eric Private Papers of Colonel Sir Eric
Gore-Browne (Documents.256)
©The Estate of Colonel Sir Eric Gore-
Browne; Photograph ©Photographer's
Estate

Herbert Private Papers of Captain
H Ward (Documents.22831)
©The Estate of Captain H Ward;
Photograph ©Photographer's Estate

Fred Private Papers of F J Murfin
(Documents.14) ©The Estate of
F J Murfin

Kit Private Papers of Vice Admiral
C Caslon (Documents.10850) ©The
Estate of Vice Admiral C Caslon;
Photograph ©Photographer's Estate

Lawrence Private Papers of Captain
L Gameson (Documents.612) ©The
Trustees of the Imperial War Museum;
Photograph ©Photographer's Estate

Bobby Private Papers of Miss G M
West (Documents.7142) ©S A West;
Photograph ©Photographer's Estate

Bert Private Papers of A L Atkins
(Documents.10767) ©The Estate of
A L Atkins; Photograph
©Photographer's Estate

Gilbert Private Papers of Sir Gilbert
Laithwaite (Documents.12262)
©Trinity College, Oxford

Arthur Private Papers of A E Wrench
(Documents.3834) ©The Estate of
A E Wrench